FREEDOM FORMULA

"Freedom begins between the ears."
— **Edward Abbey**

FREEDOM FORMULA

HOW TO GROW AN
ECOMMERCE EMPIRE

JONMAC

CROWN
Media & Printing

FREEDOM FORMULA
HOW TO GROW AN ECOMMERCE EMPIRE

© 2019 **JON MAC**

Address all inquiries to:
Jon Mac | www.JonMac.co | www.CommerceHQ.com

ISBN 978-0-578-42407-1 hardcover
ISBN 978-0-578-42408-8 eBook

Editors: Julia T. Willson, Standout Books
Cover Designer: John Walter
Interior Book Layout: Standout Books
Author Photo: Neil Slattery

Every attempt has been made to properly source all quotes.

First Edition

4 6 8 10 12 14

DEDICATION

To my love, Jacqueline, for inspiring me to stay focused and achieve my biggest life goals, dreams, and aspirations. I'm so grateful that you believed in me and never gave up.

To my business partner, Vlad at CommerceHQ, thank you for joining me on this incredible journey. Your genius, professionalism and focus have helped create an incredible company.

And to all the experts I've been mentored by in my life who've helped me become who I am today. Thank you for spending the time with me so I could grow. I owe you much of my success, for which I will be forever thankful.

"The minute you begin to do what you really want to do, it's really a different kind of life."
— **Buckminster Fuller**

CONTENTS

ACKNOWLEDGEMENTS

I've been fortunate to network with some of the smartest individuals in the industry. Their concepts, ideas, knowledge, and strategies have helped shape my success in life.

I have completed a number of training courses to boost my expertise with digital marketing, and it would be impossible to thank everyone who has helped me. But I do want to make an honorable mention of these genius marketers, who made it possible to get where I am now: Jason Akatiff, Vlad Bretgoltz, Tim Burd, Ezra Firestone, Frank Kern, Nicholas Kusmich, Sam Ovens, and everyone else who has mentored me in some form or fashion during the past ten years!

Last but not least, I'd like to thank our amazing team at CommerceHQ for all the hard work, focus, and dedication they contribute every day. All your outstanding efforts have made this book possible.

PREFACE

You're here for a reason. Something inside of you is dissatisfied. You read the news about unemployment increasing, wages stagnating, interest rates going up, and just about everything getting more expensive. Something doesn't feel right. The math doesn't work out. The system is broken and we're all trapped in it.

We're told to go school, get a university degree, get a job, buy a house, get married, and have kids. But what if the university degree puts us in huge amounts of debt? What if the jobs aren't there? What if the real estate market has skyrocketed to prices where people are either borrowing way too much on their mortgages or can't even get on the property ladder at all? More and more couples are choosing not to have expensive weddings or have kids. This is not a nightmare but our reality. The dream is broken, and it has been for a while.

You might think the solution is to work harder, put more hours in, and try to earn more. But you only have so many hours in a day. You immediately cap your income by how many hours you can humanly work. I'm saddened when I hear of people working three jobs a week for an hourly minimum wage. They will never build wealth this way. Here is a concept I want you to familiarize yourself with. Chances are, you already know this: working hourly for a wage is not scalable.

Here's what I wish we were taught in school: money needs to be made while you sleep, while you hang out with your family, while you're on vacation. The key is to automate and outsource, so that money can be made even when you aren't there. You need to set up systems that you can leave running on their own. So how do we do this? It starts with selling. What do most people think of when they think of selling? A used car salesman. Sales has a terrible reputation, but being able to sell is the most powerful skill in the world. Being able to sell doesn't look like a used car salesman anymore. That was the past. Welcome to the future. The retail industry has changed and Ecommerce is king.

The internet has opened its doors to many new industries, but I want to talk about the impact of two in particular: Ecommerce and social media. Ecommerce has been very disruptive, and for brick-and-mortar stores, it's been a death sentence. Every few months, another retail giant files for bankruptcy: Macy's, Kmart, Zellers, Toys 'R' Us, RadioShack. Just go online and type in "retail stores filing for bankruptcy." The list goes on and on. These brands ruled for decades, pricing themselves lower than all their competition, including local mom and pop shops that struggled to keep up.

The convenience and ease of online shopping means more customers are opting to shop online rather than drive to the store. They can also get access to products not available in their area. You can easily see why shopping online is becoming the preferred way to buy. Even groceries can be delivered to your door now. There are fewer and fewer reasons to leave your house.

Here's the opportunity. These big retail companies are slow-moving dinosaurs, and they're going extinct. Their advertising strategies are old school, and it will take years to train their thousands of staff how to market effectively online. Ecommerce stores have never been easier to set up for people like you and me. Mom and pop shops now have the advantage. If they can move fast and understand how to advertise online, they can come out ahead. Right now, big retail stores are starting to move their advertising budget to the online space, but their strategies aren't streamlined. Time is of the essence. You need to figure it out before they do. Finally, the playing field has been levelled. Get on the Ecommerce train now, or get left behind.

In this book, you're going to learn about the most cutting-edge methods of online marketing. The secret sauce is knowing how to generate traffic and convert that traffic into sales. And that's why social media has been such a huge game changer. It's the main way people receive information and socialize. Most of us are glued to our phones, inhaling content from Facebook, Twitter, Instagram, and Snapchat. Advertisers know they need to be where the eyeballs are. Because of social media, it's become more about branding and the experience a customer has with a company. Sales are integrated into content, into how we receive and absorb information. It's a subtle art, best when a customer doesn't feel like they're being sold to. That's marketing. So how is this done? To be able to sell something, you need to know marketing. You may not think you know marketing, but you do it every day.

At some point in life, you've marketed yourself, your services, or your products. Every day people are judging not only each other on how they look, act and speak, but how companies look, act and speak. They're posting their opinions online and sharing them within their social circles. Content can go viral overnight.

Ecommerce and social media have given you the platform to scale. We can now reach audiences in almost every corner of the world. With just an internet connection, you can get an endless supply of customers. You are no longer limited by geography and to only advertising and selling in your city. The whole world can be your marketplace. One day soon, all successful businesses will need an online presence where they can sell products. Having your website online boosts your business' visibility and gives you an advantage over the businesses that only have physical locations.

Ecommerce is growing. It's only been two years since I wrote my first book on Ecommerce, *Cash Flow for Life*, but the community has grown massively. It's been amazing to get to know so many entrepreneurs and watch them become successful. It's true that there are many ways to become an entrepreneur, but the reason Ecommerce is my favorite choice is because it's so easy to get into.

For the technophobes: you don't need to be a genius. You don't need to be a developer, coder, or programmer. There are design templates for almost everything. For those afraid of products, or who don't know what to sell, I will give you products that are already working in the marketplace. I will find you the vendors who produce them. You don't need to be a manufacturer. And with the techniques within this book, you don't need to hold inventory. For those afraid of anything else, remember, time is our most valuable asset in life. Having the ability to scale and grow your income without being tied to the number of hours you put in per day, is why Ecommerce destroys all other business models.

Don't drift through life with the cards you've been dealt. Something happened to you that made you pick up this book. Are you ready to leave the rat race and grow your Ecommerce empire?

So without wasting any more time, let's dive in.

WHAT'S INSIDE THIS BOOK?

When I started consulting, I was convinced that all entrepreneurs would need was the exact blueprint to how I achieved my success in Ecommerce, and then they would be off to the races. I went through step-by-step exactly how I set up my store, how I found products, how I found buyers through Facebook ads, and how I fulfilled orders for my customers with little financial risk. What I didn't realize was that, not only did an entrepreneur need a business blueprint, but they also needed the right mindset to be successful. During consulting calls with my students, I realized that they all struggled with the same issues: confidence, motivation, routine, and fear.

So along with an updated practical blueprint to setting up your Ecommerce store, I've added information on how to motivate yourself to keep going and never give up; to cultivate what I call 'grit.' Being an Ecommerce entrepreneur comes with its own unique set of challenges, including information about the constantly changing Facebook algorithm, and how to navigate through the ups and downs. And because the entrepreneur life can often be a lonely one, I've created Facebook groups so that you can join and talk to other like-minded Ecommerce entrepreneurs.

This book is intended for those with basic knowledge of the Facebook platform and intermediate computer literacy. I go through the step-by-step process of setting up a store and the concepts behind launching ads and optimizing them.

The best way to use this book is to read it at least twice. The first read is to familiarize yourself with the Ecommerce world and terminology. The second read is best accompanied with action. Load up the e-book version and have it on your computer, side-by-side with your store and Facebook ad account.

This book has been written in ten phases.

In Phase 1, I'll tell you about my life before and after Ecommerce.

In Phase 2, I'll explain the problems that I found with employment and how it may not be as secure as it's advertised to be.

In Phase 3, I'll go through the entrepreneur mindset. This section, I feel, was largely missing from my last book. I've realized that many students come into entrepreneurship for the wrong reasons and/or lacking the emotional skills to deal with the challenges of running their own business.

Phase 4 goes over the current state of the brick-and-mortar industry versus the Ecommerce industry. The retail industry is changing, and the effects of Ecommerce on brick-and-mortar is compelling.

From Phase 5 onwards, I get into the practicalities of setting up your online store. We'll go over what tools you'll need, and the skills you'll need to brush up on, such as law, accounting, and math.

In Phase 6, I'll take you through, step-by-step, the art of building your store. I'll explain all the elements of a successful store, including page design, apps, payment methods, emails, and upsells. Many students never get past this stage because they are perfectionists and get too distracted by their website's appearance. I have streamlined this process so that you do not get stuck and lose momentum.

In Phase 7, you'll be shown how to find proven products. One of the biggest worries for new Ecommerce entrepreneurs is what they should sell. You will learn not to get emotional over product selection and, instead, analyze what customers want, and find out what's working in the marketplace right now.

Phase 8 gets very exciting as we deep dive into the launching of ads. We'll cover everything from targeting, to identifying a winning product, to scaling out and fulfilling your orders. Watching those first sales come in is when the reality and potential of this business hits home.

Phase 9 is where we free up your time by outsourcing your tasks to virtual assistants. I show you how to find online talent and how to train them so that your business can run, even when you aren't there. This is where the freedom part of the 'Freedom Formula' happens. Whether you want to spend that extra time with family and friends or starting another business (like I did), is up to you. We all have our own definitions of freedom, but the goal is to have options.

In Phase 10, I reveal my reasons for creating CommerceHQ. Some may call me crazy, but I felt that the current Ecommerce platforms were painful to set up and not optimized for conversion. I invite you to join and follow my adventures in pushing the limits of online marketing with this revolutionary software.

So who is this book for? This book is for you if...

- You need extra income.
- You're sick of your 9–5 job and want to create a business for yourself--the amount of stress, time, and work isn't reflected in your paycheck.
- You're a stay-at-home parent who wants the flexibility to work from home and be with your kids.
- You want to get rich (not necessarily quickly or easily, but you'll get there faster).

- You're an Amazon seller and want to differentiate yourself from the ever-growing competition and race to the bottom (pricing).
- You're on Etsy or eBay and want to diversify your traffic sources.
- You're a brick-and-mortar store looking to push your products online and sell to the world, not just your town.
- You're looking to generate leads using Facebook ads for a self-employed business.
- You're already an online marketer but want to start an Ecommerce business.
- You already have an Ecommerce business and want to learn how to scale.

This book is not for you if...

- You are carrying a ton of unsecured debt.
- You are looking for a get-rich-quick scheme.
- You are lazy and don't want to do the work.
- You give up easily and move on to the next business opportunity.
- You are a perfectionist to the point that it freezes your ability to take action.
- You blame others for your failure and rarely take responsibility.

THE BAD NEWS

Some of you believe you can find success with no monetary or time investment. So even if I gave you my courses and blueprints for free, your probability of becoming successful would be very low. Achieving success in this business is not just about the information you have; it's more the state of mind you are in. This business plan is not for you if you're broke. If you're struggling to pay bills, if your bank account reads zero or worse, then entrepreneurship is not a luxury you can afford...yet. You won't have the focus or the ability to make good decisions.

Get your finances into a better position, so that when you do start your own business, it's not in a state of stress or desperation. Those of you who are trying to believe in entrepreneurship with no capital to start your business are just hoping to hit the jackpot. This is not a get-rich-quick scheme. It takes work ethic, a good attitude, and the right mindset.

Ecommerce is an easy enough business model for anyone to understand. There's no need for a university degree or any conventional schooling. But it does require focus. Make sure your life is in a state where you can put your best foot forward and achieve success. What I've noticed is that, unless people have skin in the game, they become collectors of PDFs, books, white papers, webinars, and courses. This is all fine, but in no way is any of it going to motivate them to take any real action. There will always be the next strategy, the next 'big thing,' and they will still be at square one, watching all the action-takers posting their million-dollar screenshots and asking, "Why can't I have that, too?"

You might have heard of the term *wantrepreneurs*. They want it, but they don't want to work for it. By hanging out in groups of other entrepreneurs, they hope that, somehow, success will rub off on them through osmosis. Plus, they feel productive 'learning' and socializing. But the only people they're fooling are themselves.

THE GOOD NEWS

Although Ecommerce does come with some start-up costs, it is nowhere near the cost of a brick-and-mortar retail business where you must lease a physical building, store inventory, and hire local staff. You can start your Ecommerce store with as little as a few thousand dollars and scale that up to seven figures relatively quickly. If you have a healthy and realistic outlook on Ecommerce and the entrepreneur lifestyle, you will find success. Stay away from stories that seem too good to be true or mentors who flash their cash, cars, and models. While being flashy can be a good way to catch your attention, be selective with the information you get. Dreaming of your future can be great motivation, but it can also be a great distraction. As you experience the entrepreneur lifestyle, it will open your eyes to many types of freedom; but like anything new that you learn, it's always hardest at the beginning. Once you get over that hurdle, your life will be forever changed for the better.

The entrepreneurial journey looks like this:

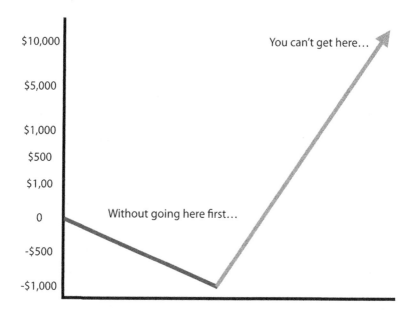

What if you stopped right before the part where the curve shoots up? Never give up. Ecommerce is a lucrative industry, and it's picking up speed. And if others can do it, so can you. Your life matters. Your happiness and the way you spend your time matters. If Ecommerce sounds like the right business for you and suits your desired lifestyle, then keep on reading.

INTRODUCTION

Holy crap. My fiancée and I were staring at our store dashboard. Our screen read $6.8 million in revenue.

In under a year.

From one store.

I had never been so excited to wake up every day. We looked forward to those stats. We looked forward to doing our ROI (Return on Investment) sheet. We looked forward to watching the money flow into our bank account daily. When you see that kind of cash rolling in, your mind races through a million things. How did we get so lucky? What are we going to buy? Is this even real? Do we even deserve this? At the end of the day, we were left with one big question: should we hide how we did it or should we share it?

There are some people in this industry who have a scarcity mindset. They find success, and they squirrel themselves away. They think that by sharing their success, someone will come and steal it. But I don't believe in that. I have an abundance mindset. Even if you find success once or twice, it's easier to find success again and again if you have a community who shares. And I never believe that I have all the answers all the time. So many people have helped me get to where I am now, and I wouldn't be here without them.

I've always felt that it's the responsibility of those who make it to send the elevator back down. I make a point to immerse myself in the Ecommerce community. We all share the same drive, the same fears, the same struggles and successes.

My life is richer because of the entrepreneurs I've met. I've always been a social person, and I believe that more heads are better than one. No successful entrepreneur does it alone, and if they said they did, they're lying. When I meet another entrepreneur, it's an amazing feeling because they just get it. They understand the lifestyle I'm striving to achieve. They understand why I left the 9 to 5 grind and entered the exciting world of entrepreneurship. Entrepreneurs don't wait for a job opening to get an income. We don't wait for a promotion or a raise. We don't want to waste our time playing the game of office politics. We're hustlers. We see opportunity everywhere, and we are not afraid to take action. My hope is that I open your eyes to the world of Ecommerce, the way it opened mine. I owe every achievement that I have to this industry and the people I've met in it. For those of you who shy away from owning a business, I never knew I could be a successful entrepreneur until Ecommerce came along. Ecommerce not only gave me the dream lifestyle, but it was, and still is, an outlet for my personality. I'm obsessive and sometimes, as my fiancée will tell me, just a bit "too much." I have a lot of energy and a lot of things I want to accomplish. I call this "entrepreneurial DNA." And if you're reading this book, chances are that you have that same obsessive entrepreneurial DNA in you.

Here's Apple's Think Different campaign from the 90s:

"Here's to the crazy ones. The misfits. The rebels. The troublemakers. The round pegs in the square holes. The ones who see things differently. They're not fond of rules. And they have no respect for the status quo. You can quote them, disagree with them, glorify or vilify them. About the only thing you can't do is ignore them. Because they change things. They push the human race forward. And while some may see them as the crazy ones, we see genius. Because the people who are crazy enough to think they can change the world are the ones who do." — Rob Siltanen

To me, this quote is talking to the entrepreneurs. We are round pegs in square holes. The ones who see opportunity to change and improve, when others fight to stay the same. The world is progressing fast. Technology is eradicating industries. From brick-and-mortar stores to anything that can be automated. Any job that can be done by a robot faces extinction. It's never been a more uncertain time to be an employee.

Entrepreneurs don't fight progress. We embrace it. And that's why we'll always come out on top. So read this book in full, because I'm about to give you a road map for how to create the lifestyle of your dreams with Ecommerce.

WHAT TO DO RIGHT NOW

I know you're busy. I'm sure you have a lot of work today. But maybe I've piqued your interest, and you are truly ready to change your life in this moment. I know you might not take immediate action with the information in this book, so I have two suggestions for you:

1. **Read the next four chapters today.**
   Right now if you can. It won't take very long. If you can commit to reading the next four chapters, you will discover what it takes to break through and achieve success in your

life. You'll hear about my story and how I overcame the 9 to 5 grind. Maybe you will relate to the workplace suffering and incredible struggles I had on my journey to seven figures.

2. **Have an open mind.**
    After consulting thousands of people over the past few years, I've realized that the only thing holding you back is yourself. You know you want more out of life. You see others who are wildly successful in Ecommerce. But nothing will change unless you truly believe it's all possible. That you can do it, too. Keep an open mind while reading this book; it could change your life forever.

PHASE ONE

THE ORIGIN STORY

THE DISCOVERY

never knew where life was going to lead me. I just followed the open doors. I learned how to separate distractions from opportunities. I had no idea that one day I would be a successful Ecommerce business owner and mentor, and that I would even create my own Ecommerce platform, CommerceHQ.

Discovering Ecommerce was like discovering myself. To say Ecommerce became an obsession is an understatement. Friends I grew up with are surprised at what I do now, and even more surprised that I found success doing it. I was one of those kids who psychologists would have diagnosed with ADHD and stuck me on Ritalin to 'level me out.' I wasn't academic, goal-oriented, or the hockey star my parents wanted me to be. Looking back I realize that I was a real mess. But to anyone who says people can't change, they're wrong. I did a total 180.

When I was a teenager, I was obsessed with house music. But not house music the way it sounds now. Back then, I listened to acid techno. You know that famous dance track in the movie *Blade*? That kind of music. My parents made me a music studio in their garage and tried to soundproof me in. They created this space because they thought it would be better for me to party at home, rather than going out all the time. It was the 90s, I was fifteen and

I wanted to be a music producer and DJ. To their dismay, I hosted parties in forests, warehouses, and 'secret locations,' but DJing gave me the experience of performing in front of large crowds, a skill I use to this day. My grades were below average because I didn't have any interests in school. I graduated high school and, even though I was by no means academic, I signed up for college.

University was a failure. Ironically, I failed the two subjects that I needed to know for business: accounting and law. I didn't learn well in a school environment. I couldn't absorb information by being lectured to without taking any practical action. My attention span was too short, and I wasn't interested in any of the subjects. I didn't have any direction in life except for my love of house music and partying which, as you can guess, didn't make me any richer.

This is where I used to live, The Green Monster.

Source: Google

I have some fond memories of this place. I remember waking up there at 3 a.m. to see a bunch of flashing lights out my window. Half awake and confused, I looked out the window left and up to the top of the building. Everyone was taking pictures of a scene below. Then I peered down and was horrified to see two young adults fornicating in the bushes. A few months later, in those same bushes, someone got stabbed. I went back there recently. Nothing has changed. The building still looks like it's about to collapse. There's cardboard, tin foil, and garbage bags on some of the windows. I've got to say, I'm very glad I don't live there now.

Because my DJing career wasn't taking off, and I needed income, my parents suggested I get into real estate. Becoming a licensed realtor was a great experience. It gave me a sneak peek into the lives of the wealthy. It taught me how to dress, how to talk, and how to sell. I did pretty well, and at the height of the market, I was selling multi-million dollar homes and earning a six-figure income. But then 2008 hit.

Going through a market crash and working in a field hit hardest by the recession sucked. One thing I've learned to this day is that you can't count on deals going through...until they do. And definitely do not spend money that you assume you will receive *before* you receive it, which is what I did. I bought a car I couldn't afford, and when I couldn't make the payments, I had to sell it. I went from driving this Cadillac...

...to this Purple Dinosaur.

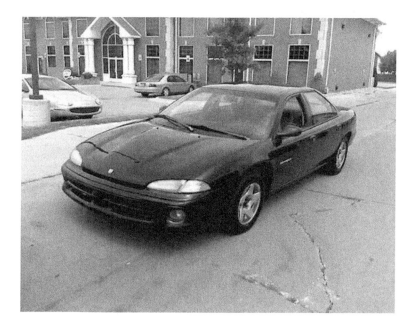

Losing the car was the least of my troubles, because I also found myself $50,000 in debt. I was twenty-three years old. Having tens of thousands of dollars in debt in your early twenties is, sadly, not uncommon. Most people finish university with huge student debt. It's a terrible way to start your journey in life. For many young adults, it's the elephant in the room that the try not to look at while trying to get ahead and make it.

The $50,000 in debt came from real estate deals falling through and from spending money I thought I would be getting before I actually had it. I was buying cars, TVs, and furniture. You know those 'buy now, pay later' schemes? I fell for those. I had stores calling me years later for money I owed them.

After the crash, I still worked as a realtor. When I met clients, I would have to park the Purple Dinosaur around the block and walk to meet them. I had to hide this piece of junk, while giving tours of mansions to wealthy clients. The business of real estate is very image-conscious. If you don't look successful, nobody wants to work with you.

One morning, I was late for a showing, trying to sell a property. I was coming up to an intersection, when suddenly my brakes failed and I plowed into the bumper of the car in front of me. Not only was I late for my showing, but I was also embarrassed to see the buyers standing on the adjacent property, watching the accident. Luckily, I hadn't met them before, so they didn't know I was the realtor. Dodged that bullet, big-time!

Going through something like this was a shock to the system. My self-esteem was crushed. My confidence flatlined. I could have sunk into a deep depression and blamed the market, blamed the clients that backed out of the deal, blamed anybody else, but me. The problem with blame and a victim mentality is that you focus on the anger and the pain of the situation instead of getting yourself out of it. It's easy to get sucked into feeling sorry for yourself. Who cares whose fault it is? You're the one who's going to have to live with it.

The looming shadow of debt loomed over my head. I won't lie–I didn't face it head on. I tried to ignore it. I distracted myself with late-night parties and drinking with friends. But at the end of the day, the debt was still waiting for me. At one point, collection agencies were calling me, and I was getting angry letters in the mail about money I owed. It was getting harder and harder to ignore. At one point, my parents told me to declare bankruptcy, but it would have destroyed my credit score so I wouldn't have been able to get a credit card for seven years. Everyone has their own moment of hitting rock bottom, and mine happened when I realized that I didn't even have $50 to my name. I had to make the mental decision to sink or swim. I decided to swim. Getting rid of the debt became a priority. The side effect of accumulating $50,000 of debt was that I became very open-minded about finding a way to pay it off. I didn't have an ego about what jobs or actions I'd have to take. I had a goal, and I was focused.

That's when I googled, 'How to make money online.' The search showed me hundreds of opportunities, and it was incredible. I learned about the affiliate industry, which is where I got my start in online marketing. I got my first taste of earning money passively when I set up an offer for people to check their credit. Every time an application was filled out, I was paid a commission. I remember going for a swim, sitting in the steam room, and coming back to money in my account. This was the life I had dreamed of. I thought I had hit the jackpot, but I hadn't discovered Ecommerce yet.

Fast forward to today–Ecommerce has paid me far more than affiliate marketing alone ever would have. The online marketing world is evolving into the legitimate and sophisticated Ecommerce industry. It has changed my life for the better in every way. When

I think back and remember being in such a dark place, it fuels me every day to succeed. I'm never going back to that time. I don't want to feel being hopeless or broke ever again. I take full responsibility for the decisions I made leading up to that point in my life. I was living beyond my means and didn't have the income to support it. In hindsight, the recession was the best thing to happen to me. It snapped me out of dreamland and got me focused on my finances.

The lessons you learn from complete and utter failure are like no other. If you've faced failures, don't pretend they never happened—learn from them. Adapt. Change. Grow. Let them inform your decisions today. I doubt anyone thought I was going to amount to much, including me. There are days when I still feel like I could have worked harder or accomplished more. That drive to prove myself is always there. When you're hustling hard, you don't take the time to smell the roses. My fiancée and I often have to force ourselves to step back and look at our lives. When we compare where we were to where we are now, we don't even realize how much everything has changed.

The life of bosses, raises, promotions and paid holiday time is gone. The life of working hourly for a wage, or struggling to pay off debt…gone. Today, we get to choose when and where we want to work, when we go on vacation, and how we want to live. The potential amount of income that Ecommerce provides can change your life in a heartbeat. You won't even know what hit you.

THE WORKPLACE WAR ZONE

've had some interesting experiences working for other people. And by interesting, I mean dangerous! I almost died, I was harassed, and physically attacked. It was a war zone. Here are some of my favorite memories from when I was an employee. And, by favorite, I mean *really* messed up.

When I was young, I lived in Vancouver and worked many odd jobs. One of them was installing skylights in multimillion-dollar homes with my best friend. Let me preface this by saying that I am not a handy person. Although I come from a family of very handy blue-collar relatives, I did not inherit this skill. It was truly inspiring working on these mansions, but the job itself was incredibly treacherous. One time, when I was on a roof, thirty feet up in the air, installing this massive skylight. It was raining, as it typically does in Vancouver, and we were on a strict timeline. Our job was to finish the installation that day. At some point, I lost my grip, my feet slid out from underneath me, and I started hurtling toward the edge of the house. At the last possible moment, before I flew off the edge of the roof, I managed to stick my foot in the gutter system and save myself from falling to my death. My short life could have ended right then and there.

Shortly after this incident, our boss decided not to pay us. He said he would make it up to us in the next paycheck. Week after week, he gave the same excuse. We never saw the money. We later found out that he had been taking weekend trips to Vegas and gambling with our hard-earned money. When we confronted him about it, he said he was going to give us a big bonus if he won. Needless to say, I quit that job.

When I was in my twenties, I dabbled in online marketing and made extra income. This side hustle turned into a real career, and I got a job as a media buyer for a top affiliate-marketing company. This company was publicly traded and was very profitable in its day. Unfortunately, its best days were gone, because it was under new management that drove the company into the ground.

I attended daily scrum meetings in a corporate-style boardroom with a co-worker that would be sexually inappropriate who, coincidentally, was my boss. He would reminisce about his failures in the bedroom with his lover, while we tried to concentrate on growing the company. Unsurprisingly, the company didn't grow and got into deep financial trouble. I quit before it went bankrupt. The day I quit ended with my boss chasing me down the stairs, begging me to stay.

The next job was even worse. One of my co-workers was a large, angry man with the appearance and temperament of a raging bull. He was the big shot at the office. He had the most accounts and clients, which meant that although he was rude and crass, he was also untouchable. One day, while we were enjoying a glass of wine on a Friday afternoon at the office, someone bumped into me and I accidentally spilled some of my wine on the raging bull. He overreacted, as expected, and was pissed off. He went to the washroom to clean up but shortly returned with a vengeance.

As he approached me, I saw anger in his eyes, and I knew something was about to go down. The next thing I knew, I was thrown up against the wall, a fist in my face and the other hand holding my collar. One thing I am not is a fighter. I stared at him in shock and waited for the first blow, tensing my muscles, anticipating the hit. Seconds later, our manager came running out of the office to break it up.

Luckily for me, the whole encounter was captured on video surveillance. He was done. The next day, I had Human Resources and lawyers contacting me, making sure I wasn't going to sue the company. I realized they had no concern for my wellbeing and were only worried about the company's reputation. Had the video not surfaced, I believe they would have debated and negotiated how to keep this guy employed. Thankfully, there was no way anyone could dispute what had happened, and the raging bull was fired. As for me, there was no compensation, no time off, no sympathy, and the next week was business as usual.

I'd love to say that I remember those days with fondness; the things you put up with to get a regular paycheck. I'm sure you have horror stories of your own. It's just sad that so many people have gone through some sort of workplace war zone. Putting dissatisfied, competitive, and desperate people on a team is a recipe for disaster.

THE GREAT ESCAPE

One of the most satisfying memories I have is the day I quit that job; from announcing my resignation, to the look on my boss' face, to packing up my things and walking out the door. That day is one I will cherish forever. Quitting happened in an instant, but getting to that point felt like a lifetime.

I was still working as a media buyer in Toronto. The salary was okay—Just enough to keep me trapped, but I wasn't happy there. I didn't like my colleagues and the city was a concrete jungle. Everything— the late-night lifestyle, the traffic, and the small condos—got old fast. I was living for Fridays and hated the workweek. Being stuck in this hamster wheel didn't make sense, so I started looking for a way out.

I had never forgotten the first success I had online, selling credit reports. I was hooked. So I was determined to find a way to be my own boss. It wasn't a regular income, so I still needed a regular job, but I knew that online marketing was going to be my ticket out. Even when I was working 9 to 5, I never stopped the side hustle. I was always online, looking for opportunities to create my own income stream. And then I stumbled across a custom t-shirt platform called: Teespring. It was a platform that handled all the fulfillment.

You just had to design the t-shirt, send traffic, and make sales. They charged you for the cost of the product and the shipping. You paid for the ads. You chose the price of the shirt, and if it was above the cost of fulfillment and ads, you made a profit.

Facebook ad strategies were pretty simple back then. For example, to sell a firefighter shirt, I would target 'firefighters,' and get awesome results. Getting 200% ROI from sales on this site was not uncommon, and there was little competition. It was like printing money.

Source: teespring.com

In-between my boss' walks around the office, I would research designs, hire designers to create the artwork, and launch t-shirt campaigns. Once, my boss caught me looking at t-shirts, and I awkwardly pretended I was shopping. I thought it would be better for him to think that I was buying a shirt instead of working on my escape plan. I made sure that I was still doing my work duties. In fact, I was earning the company millions of dollars and outperforming most of my colleagues. That made me angry. I was spending all my time building up someone else's company, yet my commission was embarrassing.

The feeling of wanting to quit is powerful. You start hating everyone and everything. Every minute you spend in the office feels like a waste of time. You can never get it back. All you think about is how to escape employment. My girlfriend (now fiancée) told me not to quit until I had six months of consistent income and was confident I could turn this into a real business. We had learned not to shoot ourselves in the foot by relying on income we didn't have yet. As hard as it was for me to stay at the company, we made sure that we had a solid exit plan before we considered putting any ideas into motion.

Around the six-month mark, I wanted to go to Vancouver. I had vacation time saved up, and I was also due to see a lawyer to deal with a past issue with a car accident. But my boss didn't want me to go for two weeks; he only approved one week. I was furious. I disobeyed orders and stayed in Vancouver for two weeks. When it became clear to my boss that I was taking the unapproved extra week off without permission, he sent an email saying we "would have to talk." But my six months were up, and now I was making more per month than I was at my job. When I got back to the office, I was nervous, but excited. The time had finally come. This is how one of the best moments of my life transpired:

My boss said, "I need to talk to you."

And I said, "Actually, I need to talk to YOU."

Within a matter of seconds, I unshackled myself from his authority. I quit. His face went bright red. He was speechless. I left the room, packed up my desk, and left. And that was the last time I had—and will ever have—a boss.

THE ECOMMERCE REVOLUTION

For me, escaping the 9 to 5 was a rebellion against the need to be 'employed.' It represented the ability to question every preconception we had been taught about earning an income, financial stability, and getting wealthy. The transition from employee to employer opened my eyes to a world full of opportunity. As an employee, you are forced to turn away from opportunities to help yourself. The company comes first; your needs are secondary if considered at all. Any business dreams end up getting pushed to one side and rarely looked at again. This is the life that we have all been sold.

We try the traditional route of education, and some people can do well in this system. But most of us don't. Most of us don't even need to go to university. Universities became greedy. They started selling us the need for degrees. And, with that, came debt. Credit card companies would offer their services to students on campuses who didn't know any better. These predatory acts would lead to people spending years attempting to pay off their debt. You cannot default on student loans…period. They haunt you until you pay them off. I have friends who have gone back to university to get another degree. The problem when everyone is getting degrees is that it's hard to differentiate yourself from the competition. So you go back and get a master's degree, incur more debt, and still have no guarantee of a job at the end of it. And if you do land the elusive 9 to 5 dream job, (though you probably work longer hours than that), you're in the rat race. You're on the career ladder. You're in the system. And if you want to earn more, there's very little you can do about it.

As someone who owns his own business, I have full control of my life. It feels like I'm on the outside of a goldfish bowl. I'm looking in, watching people fight over promotions, raises, and vacation time. I watch them get told when to eat and when it's okay to have a coffee break. Every movement, action, and word are monitored. There are so many redundant rules and ways to keep you in line. Productivity isn't even a priority; it's more knowing your place. What a strange way to live. But because most people live this way, it seems normal. Office politics have become a foreign concept to me. I don't have colleagues I don't like. I hire who I want and I fire who I don't want. I'm able to surround myself with the exact people I want to be around and work closely with.

My parents once told me that all I needed to do was earn enough to pay the bills. That getting wealthy was a pipe dream. What do you need that stress for? Have a simple life, keep your head down, and pay your bills. There's nothing like a regular paycheck. The past generation dreams of retirement and their pensions. They do things like play the lottery. "Just gotta hit the jackpot once," they say. What a waste of time, waiting around for life to just hand you millions of dollars. Do you want to wait until you're sixty-five to start living your life? But your job is stable right? Wrong. As more and more companies 'restructure,' people get fired, and that regular paycheck disappears. The job you think is so stable could get ripped out from under you at any time. Do you really want someone else to be in control of something as important as your income? Companies aren't loyal to you. They're loyal to their bottom line. And if they have to fire you in order to stay afloat, they will...without hesitation.

But there's another option: build your own business. The secret is out. There are kids making millions on YouTube. People in their twenties and thirties are making apps and selling them for millions and even billions. I think that kind of income and wealth scares some people. They aren't ready for it. They don't believe it's even a possibility for them. But there's a mass movement happening. Entrepreneurship should not be that rare career choice that people look at with fear and shake their heads at. It should be seen as the only option. The online world has given our generation an enormous opportunity, not only to earn income beyond our neighborhoods, but also beyond country borders. Owning your own business is especially important, because there is no such thing as job security. It's never been easier to search for jobs and work online. The entire world becomes your job hunting and hiring pool. All you need is a laptop and an internet connection.

Right now, we have ten staff members in the Philippines. We built an office for them and bought all the equipment. Our business model connected us to talented people across the planet, who we otherwise would never have met. Not to mention, the benefit of the currency exchange is great for both them and us. Ecommerce is more than just a great income source. It challenges every traditional way of earning income. No need for a résumé or meeting prerequisites to get hired. No need for a boss. No need to wait for a promotion or holiday time. It even stands in the face of what we think we need when starting a business. There's no need for investors. No need for inventory or a warehouse. No need for local staff. You can be a one-man or one-woman show and earn six or even seven, figures in a relatively short amount of time.

This is the Ecommerce revolution.

THE LIFE-CHANGING MOMENT

When I try to think of a moment when my life changed, it's hard to pick one. There are so many experiences I get to have that a 9–5er could never understand. Quitting my job would be the most obvious choice, but how about this moment?

This is a $6.8 million-dollar screenshot from just one of my Ecommerce stores. It blew my mind when I saw the earning potential of Ecommerce. But was it just luck? Right time, right place? I wanted to see if I could help my students and get them to replicate success using my methods.

Here are two examples of people who I've helped succeed with Ecommerce:

Isabel Pizarro is 😌 feeling proud.
November 17, 2017 · 🌐

Woa. Today I hit 1 MILIION DOLLARS in Sales!! 😱😌 Timeframe: exactly 6 months. My initial goal for this store I opened in May was to hit $100,000 by the end of the year. Crazy. 😅 When I realized I was kicking ass more than I anticipated, I raised my goal to slay 1 Mil by the end of the year and here I am, 6 weeks early! Eekkkk. 😆 Super freaking proud of myself... 💪 What a journey it has been, phew! A roller coaster of emotions that's for sure! Lots of obstacles. 🩸 Blood 💦 Swe... See More

TRENDS 24H 1W 1M 3M CUSTOM

Revenue $1,008,551.61 Orders Visitors 739,573

ISABEL PIZARRO

Love   Comment   Share

You, Isabel Pizarro, Jonas Hedegaard and 168 others

These are seven-figure screenshots from my students. The fact that not only could I earn seven figures with Ecommerce, but that I could teach others to do so as well, is an amazing feeling. Helping others change their lives is one of the most rewarding experiences I've had.

Jonas Hedegaard
March 17 at 11:13am   ...

2018 has been crazy so far 🤞 We just hit the $2M Mark and just opened
this store in the middle of September Last Year 👍

We really scaled hard in March and were able to hit over $1M in Revenue
the last 30 days Alone 🔥

What I learned the last few weeks:
- Scale hard on your winning adsets and kill the loosing adsets FAST!
- Have a strong DPA Setup (Crazy ROAS)
- Make sure to have a really Strong Backend when scaling
- Have your abandoned Cart sequence optimized - will really bring a lot
of your customers back to your store to purchase

And if you still use Shopify... Then switch to CommerceHQ ASAP ! We
would have been paying crazy high app costs and Shopify fees with this
revenue 😅

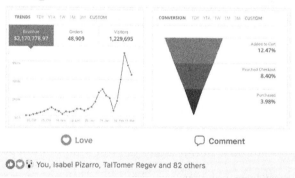

⭕ Love   💬 Comment

👍❤️😮 You, Isabel Pizarro, TalTomer Regev and 82 others

At one of my live event seminars, a student of mine started implementing the strategies that I was teaching him, during the work-
shop. The kid was just twenty-one years old and very driven. He
didn't sleep and worked all night because he wanted success badly.
The event was over three days and here were his results:

Day 1: He launched products he found at the event, using my
Ecommerce strategies. The first day, he hit $800 in revenue.
Day 2: He started scaling his winners and made $5,000 in revenue
the next day.

Day 3: For the last day, we were on a boat, celebrating Canada Day with all my other students.

He took out his phone, which he had hooked up to his Ecommerce dashboard, and it read $30,000. Shortly after, fireworks went off in the night sky. Perfect timing.

Two days later, he messaged me with a screenshot. He had hit $83,000 in just one day alone. Now, these results are not typical at all, but they show the potential of Ecommerce. His story was not isolated. Other students were doubling and tripling their revenue in just a few days at the event. Minds were blown. Eyes were opened. Lives were changed. And we were just getting started. It solidified Ecommerce as the biggest game changer for any online entrepreneur.

This is the real deal.

Ecommerce has changed the way I think. I think about my time differently. I think about what I value in life differently. And I think about money differently. Back when I started using Facebook ads, spending $500 a day made me sick. Now I don't even blink when I spend $5,000. When you start spending $20K, $40K, $100K per day, the numbers are just math to you. As long as you're making it back and more, it doesn't faze you. Ecommerce allows you to scale your business and increase your income exponentially and without limitations. You don't have to wait for a promotion to earn more. If you're tired, you can go play golf or take some time off. There's no one to tell you 'no.'

The great thing about entrepreneurship is that it's constantly bettering your life. Ecommerce has been my golden ticket to amazing, unique and once-in-a-lifetime experiences. If you've been following my Instagram or Facebook stories, the big thing this year is that we're building our dream home. Because my business is online, I get to live anywhere. As long as I have a good internet connection, I'm golden.

I used to live in Toronto, but it's a concrete jungle and I'm a nature boy. Deep down, I wanted trees, mountains, and water. I wasn't happy living in the city. So we moved to BC. My fiancée and I talk about lifestyle design. What did we want our lives to look like? When we thought about it, we both knew we wanted a big house, a beautiful view, and a stress-free environment. We wanted somewhere we could come back to, after all our adventures together, that would be our home, our retreat, and our spa. Our own piece of paradise.

While walking the dog, we stumbled across this beautiful lot facing the lake. It was the last lot for sale on the mountain. We bought it on the spot. Never in my wildest dreams would I have thought I would be able to say, "I'll take it!" for a piece of land with such a stunning view.

Earning a big income is one thing, but watching it physically change your life for the better, is another. You don't see a lifestyle change when money just sits in your bank account. But when we converted those digital numbers on a screen into buying our lot and building our dream home, a home we could live in and grow in, we truly understood the power of Ecommerce.

I think the biggest way that Ecommerce will change my life hasn't even arrived yet. It will be at the end of this year, when the house is built, and I can finally move in with my family.

ACTION PROMPTS

1. If you have a full-time job and are serious about entrepreneurship, this is the time to start crafting your vision. What will your life look like in one year, five years, ten years? How do you want to shape your future so that you are the one in control, commanding your destiny? Write down what you want your life to look like. Then continue reading this book.

2. If you are a student in college or university, do you have a plan to get out of debt? Will you bow to the system and follow what most people do? Go to school, get a job, retire at sixty-five and hope you have enough for retirement? That's the old way. Keep reading to find out about the 'new way,' and how you can escape.

3. If you are an entrepreneur but can't seem to break through your income goals, then continue reading this book. It's filled with real world, practical strategies, tips, and techniques for getting more out of your marketing campaigns. It doesn't matter what you are selling or offering, the

information in this book will help you build, launch, and scale your business fast. I'm holding nothing back, so get ready and read on.

THE PROBLEM WITH EMPLOYMENT

THE BIGGEST LIE

Having a true entrepreneur mindset means rejecting the employee mindset, which starts infiltrating our thoughts from a young age. It starts in school, when we're young, and teaches us to trust and listen to authority figures. You trust the system that you're in and believe that everything will work out. Everyone else is following the same system, so how can everyone be wrong? School, university, job, house, family, success, happiness. This is how it's supposed to go. I wish it were true that most people found success this way. But I look around, even in my immediate circle, and see people unhappy in employment, paid too little, or not even able to find a job. People are living paycheck to paycheck, putting up with crazy office politics, and waiting for a promotion that never seems to come soon enough, if at all.

Sometimes it takes a shocking event to happen before you wake up and say enough is enough. I woke up in 2008. The 2008 market crash is still fresh in my mind. It was the glitch in the Matrix. The seed was planted in my mind that the system was broken, and it would break again. It threw my life and the lives of many others into a state of chaos, and I felt I had no control. It was only a decade ago, but the mainstream media and politicians these days are still pushing the same garbage that got us into the recession in the first place. Everything is fine. Trust the government, trust the media, trust the stock market; the only way is up. I don't see the recovery. There's a disconnect between what the mainstream media is reporting and what is actually happening. I look around and don't see economic improvement. Real estate is sky-high, wages are still stagnant, and inflation is pushing up the prices on everything from groceries to movie tickets.

Most people are just getting used to having less or getting used to having more debt. The system is rigged. It doesn't want you to build wealth. It is the most elaborate subscription program. They want you to acquire debt that they know you will never pay off. They get a steady stream of interest payments, which means they own you now. Businesses are profiting from people with debt, making easy money from easy targets. Debt collectors, refinancers, loan sharks—they smell blood in the water. Go to school, get good grades, and the house and family will just fall into place. Let's dive into these lies, one by one.

LIE #1: GO TO UNIVERSITY AND YOU'LL GET A GREAT JOB.

University is a business and a very profitable one at that. It's expensive. As a Canadian, I think the cost of tuition is overpriced in Canada. But my American friends have to take on more debt. They bank on it paying out in higher-salaried professions, but there isn't a job guaranteed at the end of it.

To make matters worse, you can't default on student debt. This could cripple you for life. What's the ROI of your degree? Are you guaranteed a job or salary raise? If you aren't, how will you pay it back? As a business owner, I think it seems like a terrible investment. The risk is much higher than the reward. Employers are also in on it. They won't hire you unless you have a degree. So we're all rushing around to build up our résumés and buy more degrees that make us look more appealing to employers.

LIE #2: YOU HAVE JOB SECURITY.

I think most of us witnessed or experienced the effects of the 2008 recession. I was personally thrown into more debt than I had ever experienced, and I was only twenty-three. My life was just getting started. Employment data is skewed. When they tell you unemployment is decreasing, they define part-time work as being employed. The gig economy is increasing, but those aren't steady jobs. Also, these reports do not consider people who are not actively seeking jobs or the ones who are homeless and have given up.

LIE #3: WORK HARD AT YOUR JOB AND YOU WILL BE REWARDED.

Most 9–5ers will tell you that they started their jobs with excitement but, as time passed, they became jaded and indifferent. This is because jobs get worse over time. Putting in more time and effort does not necessarily mean more reward. Then you're waiting until the end of the year. Waiting until your performance review. Waiting until the business is doing better. Just waiting, always. Waiting until a position opens. That person with the position you want is going to hold onto it for dear life. You'll have to wait until they quit or retire. At some point, you'll stop believing it will ever happen. You've outgrown your position, you need more income, and the job is a daily grind. It's not as stimulating and interesting to you anymore. You're bored. But you still have to keep your head down and be a team player. So you switch off. This is when you become jaded. You've realized that working harder doesn't mean more recognition or reward. You stop trying. It's just a job to you now. With entrepreneurship, it's the opposite. The struggle is at the beginning, and the success is at the end. You constantly feel challenged and, when you do succeed, there are real rewards.

LIE #4: DEBT IS MONEY.

Debt is imprisonment. Banks send representatives to go to university campuses to sign students up for credit cards. Credit card debt is one of the worst kinds of debt, with insane interest rates if you don't pay the balance off monthly. Did you know that a national bank can charge up to 80% interest rate on a credit card as long as they disclose their terms and that it is completely legal? Debt is a subscription program. I believe the banks are trying to remove our ability to build wealth. They give out cheap cash at low interest rates for mortgages, so that buying a home seems irresistible. But you've just signed up for a lifetime supply of interest payments.

LIE #5: YOU'LL BE ABLE TO SAVE.

With inflation going up every year, it's hard to keep up. Savers become the suckers. For every $100,000 you save, inflation decreases its value or purchasing power by about $3,000 per year. It forces you to take risks and invest in either stocks or real estate just to break even. A real struggle for any successful business owner is, "Okay, I've made a lot of cash. Now how do I keep it?" Everyone is out for your money.

Taxes are a headache. In Canada, we pay approximately 50% personal income tax at the top tier. This means, for every million dollars I take for myself, the government takes almost one million, too. For my American friends, the top tax tier is 37% percent. Having a tax strategy becomes a priority, but it isn't cheap. The financial services you'll be paying for include lawyers, accountants, bookkeepers, and insurance brokers. Being able to save is harder than ever. And it's being done by design.

LIE #6: YOU'LL HAVE A GOOD PENSION.

I honestly don't know if my generation will ever have a pension. And, even if we do, it will be so small it won't matter. I can't bank my future on that. When I had a paycheck in Canada, they took money out without my permission and put it toward my pension. I don't trust the system, and I'd rather take matters into my own hands and invest that money my way.

People with an entrepreneur mindset know these things. That is why we are so driven to escape this system and build a life we control. We don't want to be a drone in a hive or cog in a machine. We want to create, innovate, improve, and produce. We want to build wealth and make a better life for ourselves. If you've been hurt by these things and want to make a change, start working on your escape plan.

THE HARMFUL WORKPLACE

You know what doesn't make sense? People who think that working 9 to 5 is the safest option. When your life is in the hands of someone who could fire you, demote you, or promote you at any time, you are not in control of your destiny. I think that is the most unsafe way to live.

Entrepreneurs get it right. They know that the safest bet is to believe in, and rely on, themselves for an income. There is no such thing as job security. There is no such thing as a company being loyal to you. They don't care about whether you have bills to pay or a family to feed. They're a business and they only understand profit.

The modern workplace can cause terrible levels of stress—to the point where it becomes dangerous. The media is constantly reporting the health crises of workplaces, where employees suffer from mental illnesses like depression or anxiety and, in the worst cases, suicide. In 2016, an Uber software engineer killed himself, and his family blamed it on workplace stress. The workplace is making people sick. Quality of life suffers when you work long hours. It affects your mental and physical health and creates conflict within your family. And none of this makes sense from a financial point of view either. Studies show that working longer hours does not equal more productivity. In fact, it negatively affects it. The American Institute of Stress reports that workplace stress costs the American economy around $300 billion a year, because employees are getting chronically ill.

Your life should improve over time. When most people start a 9 to 5 job, they are excited and driven to work hard. But soon, they become jaded as they realize that working harder, or doing better, doesn't always mean getting ahead. It means someone else is getting ahead. There are few rewards for an employee. After all, they're replaceable.

This is the path for most people. It's comfortable, it's known. But the end result is always the same. You spend your whole life dedicated to someone else's company and vision. It's challenging and scary to jump on the entrepreneur train, but I think it's scarier to spend a lifetime accepting mediocrity. Time is an asset. You can never get it back.

With entrepreneurship, specifically Ecommerce, life gets exponentially better over time. At the beginning, there's a learning curve. There's definitely a struggle as your brain adjusts to thinking for itself. You've been told what to do for so long, but now you call the shots. But it's also exciting as you know that, every time you learn, every time you achieve, it's for you. And no one else. It works far better to keep you incentivized. Work hard and you get rewarded. Makes sense, right? Work to live. Don't live to work.

When I had a 9 to 5 job, my health suffered greatly. I spent my free time drinking and partying to distract myself from my unhappiness. My back pain was so bad that I had to see a massage therapist for weeks just to get back into alignment. Emotionally, I was broken. There was no light at the end of the tunnel--just mundane daily tasks that seemed to drone on forever. When you aren't inspired, life can be a very lonely existence. I've also had friends who were injured on the job and out of work for months at a time. A lot of companies couldn't care less about your health or wellbeing for that matter. But they make a huge mistake with that mindset, because employees are so much more productive and perform at higher levels when they're happy and have meaning in their lives.

One thing is for sure, no one will care more about you than yourself. And you can't help others in this life unless you help yourself first. Learn the skills now to better every area of your life, so you don't fall into the trap of living someone else's. Ecommerce is the way to get you there.

Buckle in because, in the next chapter, I'm going to explain why you need to stop being a consumer and start being a seller.

THE NEED TO SELL

L et's undo the programming. With robots and automation taking over jobs like driving, cashiers, and transport, it's more important than ever to utilize our biggest strength as humans—our individuality. You need to produce *and* sell. Whether it's products, services, or content, you must sell something. At job orientations, we were taught to follow rules and not to question them. We weren't taught to look at a situation, see how others did it, and then improve on it. We have dress codes at school and at work. We are taught to conform, keep our heads down, and be constantly graded on our performance.

But people can be inventive and original. It's a shame we don't encourage independent thinking more often and celebrate differences. The world is being designed for efficiency, but that means we lose creativity. There are studies on how schooling is breeding the creativity out of us from a young age. Being able to think for yourself and not take everything at face value is a very important quality for an entrepreneur. After all, you take the lead. We are taught to buy, not sell. There's nothing wrong with buying things, but without selling something, you will just be a consumer, not a producer. There's a reason we were taught this. Look at all the businesses profiting from your buying habits.

Source: Google

These massive big box stores don't need any more profit. They've been around for decades and have had a monopoly on the marketplace. With Ecommerce and social platforms allowing us to brand ourselves, it's time to take a piece of that pie for yourself. The field is levelling with Ecommerce. Learn how to sell and how to market now.

We're also taught that we need things like venture capitalists (VCs), or huge amounts of funding, to become an entrepreneur. That's not true at all. You can get VCs at the beginning if you want, but you can also self-fund or bootstrap your business.

Watching *Shark Tank* and *Dragon's Den*, you'd think that was the only way to get exposure. To get funding, the business owners give away a ton of equity. If you're looking for traffic, leads, or sales, you just need to figure out how to market online.

ACTION PROMPTS

1. Invest in alternative education and training, and experience what it takes to be an entrepreneur. Take two hours from each day to work on your own self-development. Put down the remote, Netflix, or other distractions and begin the learning process.

2. Can you sacrifice at least one hour per day to read this book? You will see case studies from people with real Ecommerce businesses. How they went from zero to six and even seven figures in just a few months. Now is the time to learn, strategize and take action.

3. Are you happy in your current employment? Can you relate to any of these feelings of dissatisfaction or unhappiness? Your time is valuable. Take the time to have a look at your life and figure out if you're on the path you want to be on.

PHASE THREE

THE ENTREPRENEUR MINDSET

THE FOUNDATION
OF A BUSINESS

As I write this book, we are building our dream house. I've noticed that there are lots of parallels between the practicalities of building a house and building an Ecommerce business. The concrete foundation gives the house a sturdy base. It strengthens the walls and gives the house its shape.

In Ecommerce, the foundation is *you*. Your beliefs and self-image are the foundation on which you build your thoughts and actions. You can't put a roof on a house without the foundation and walls. In Ecommerce, you can't be successful unless you have an entrepreneurial mindset.

It starts with adjusting expectations for yourself and your business. Overnight successes are rare and, in a lot of cases, are false advertising. The gurus who tell these get-rich-quick stories are preying on the weak-minded and the people who believe that success can be achieved without hard work. Everyone wants to find a shortcut. These gurus know that deep down, people are lazy. But if it sounds too good to be true, then it probably is.

We all carry self-limiting beliefs that we've learned somewhere. And most of that comes from the belief that holding onto your identity is essential. In an alternate universe, I'm probably still partying, still in debt, and still secretly very unhappy. I fought so hard to keep that lifestyle, because that's who I believed I was.

House music was my first passion. I gave it up to pursue Ecommerce, because I knew it was an opportunity of a lifetime. I knew it would provide me with the luxuries I would otherwise not be able to experience. If I hadn't let go of being a music producer, I wouldn't have the success I have today. People can get stuck on what they will or won't do, because of who they've decided they are. They say they can't change. But I'm living proof that you can, and that you should change now. Especially if it means improving your life. Don't get attached to your identity. It's self-sabotage. Don't get fixated on who you are or who you aren't. Maybe you don't believe you're a marketer. Maybe you don't believe you're an entrepreneur. Is holding onto these beliefs more important than the successful life you could be leading? Be open-minded.

Today, I'm living life to the fullest. Ecommerce has opened my life up to so many opportunities. In the future, I plan to open my own music studio and start a record label. I feel confident and relaxed knowing that I don't have to wait for someone to give me the opportunity. I can fund the project myself. This is freedom, and I hope one day you experience it, too.

In the next few chapters, we're going to dive head first into motivation and mindset. Without being mentally strong, your Ecommerce journey will always fail. Your brain is a muscle, and exercising it daily will help you succeed in business. I'm going to be covering multiple topics to help get you in the right mindset. Because if you doubt yourself and stop taking action, or you get stuck and stop progressing, nothing will work. The dream will be lost. Developing a strong mindset is the foundation of being a successful entrepreneur. The drive and strength to win against all odds will propel you forward, day after day. You will never give up. You will be focused. You will win!

THE ENTREPRENEUR LIFE

Like any experience, the entrepreneur life requires that you actually experience it to know its ins and outs. Being an Ecommerce entrepreneur is a very unique experience, and people often get into it with misguided expectations. When you think of the entrepreneur life, what images come to mind? Does it look like this?

Source: Google

The message a lot of Ecommerce gurus send out is that they made their money overnight. They hit the jackpot. They won the lottery. And oh yeah, you can do it too. It looks like immediate success, but a lot of things need to line up for success to happen. They don't show the blood, sweat, and tears behind it. They don't show the sacrifice. They don't show the full picture.

Why do they do this? The idea of turning your life around and getting rich overnight is easier to sell than creating a real business plan that you have to work at. Watching these gurus parade their wealth around is entertainment, but nothing more. Snap out of it, and come back down to Earth. Being an entrepreneur is not a spectator sport.

If you want to be successful, you must sacrifice. Sacrifice means not living the ordinary life. When people are watching football, or Netflix and chilling, or going to the pub, you'll be scaling your business. You'll be laying the groundwork for the future. This is what the real Ecommerce entrepreneurial life looks like.

The first step to becoming an entrepreneur is adjusting your expectations. Have a realistic idea of what your life is going to look like, because you're going to have to hustle for it. When you first start out, your life isn't going to magically improve. If you don't have the systems in place that earn you a consistent income, and the mindset to keep motivated, you will struggle to keep going. Here are some pros and cons of being an entrepreneur:

Pros

- You can work whenever you want and take holidays off without asking for permission.
- You can make way more money than a traditional employee.
- You don't have to wait for a raise or promotion if you want to make more.
- You are the boss.
- Your mindset changes so you see opportunities everywhere; your world expands so you figure out how to earn income in so many ways.
- You experience massive personal growth.
- You have pride in ownership and/or creation.
- You create something that is yours.
- You have purpose.

Cons

- You have a lack of routine, unless you set it.
- You feel pressure to work and get your systems in place or else there is no income.
- You feel short-term pain when you first start out.
- There is more risk and struggle.
- You may end up with a phone or laptop addiction.

- There is no work/play distinction, and your life will lack balance.
- People in your life may say that you are obsessed with your business.

I'm an obsessive person by nature, so I always need to keep busy and I struggle with balance. When I don't have a clear schedule during the day; family life and work life can blend together. This is probably the biggest con to being an entrepreneur. Instead of quality time with your spouse or friends, you may find yourself talking constantly about your business. But if you surround yourself with people who understand the sacrifice, they can adapt to your lifestyle.

The pros far outweigh the cons to me. When I think back on my 9 to 5 job, even during the most stressful of times, I think, "No way. I will never go back and will never have to."

Think about what type of business leader you want to be. Be true to yourself and identify your strengths and your weakness. Where do you excel and where do you need help? The best leaders are the ones without giant egos, people who do not insist they are always right. They are curious and open to learning every day. They understand that everyone—poor or rich, academic or street smart, introverted or extroverted—has something to teach them. And they don't just do it for themselves. One of the biggest motivators for me is doing it for my family and helping other entrepreneurs. You might want to help your community, solve a problem, or make the world a better place. Don't create a business where you're going to get ahead by screwing everyone else over. Produce something of value and be proud of it.

THE ACCUMULATION
OF WEALTH

We're taught that wanting to accumulate wealth is greedy and selfish. But ask yourself what wealth means to you. Is money good or bad? Does it mean that you're shallow and superficial, or can it instead mean that you want more time with your family, or that you want the freedom to travel and explore the world? Your opinion about money is very important, because if you have a negative relationship with it, you will never become wealthy.

Some people say rich people are evil, and they worship the 'money god,' but that's simply nonsense. You see, people usually only get rich when they produce something of real value by helping others solve a serious problem in their lives. Don't fall into the mindset trap that all people who got rich must have screwed people over somehow. That's simply an excuse for some to give up on life, their dreams, and their future, and to live in a world of mediocrity. Money is not good or bad; it's neutral. You are the only one who can be good or bad. Money is just a tool, and you decide what to do with it and how to use it.

I didn't have a lot of money growing up, and maybe that's why it's so important to me today. I always tried to live the high life but never had the income to support it. Now I can walk into any store and buy anything I desire, without getting stressed about it. The funny thing is, I'm never tempted anymore to impulse buy like I did before, when I was broke.

My hyperactivity could have been bad news. It depends on where you focus your energy. If I didn't have my business, and I was left to my own devices, I would still be partying, spending all my money on clothes and cars. My business, customers, and fiancée keep me in line and allow me to afford the lifestyle of my dreams.

Nothing is worse than living outside your means. There's nothing wrong with wanting more. But you must be able to afford it. When you aren't living within your means, you become a burden to others and stress yourself out. Whatever you want in life, go earn the money for it first, before you buy it. After you find success, you may be tempted to purchase fancy things like expensive sports cars or designer clothes. This is the absolute wrong thing to do. You must invest your profits wisely in vehicles that grow your capital and appreciate. Focus on real estate and stocks for stable growth over ten years—minimum. Your goal should be to double your investments within the same time period. I'm no pro when it comes to investments (yet), but here are a few basic rules I've learned about what to do with your money, once you've made it.

Rental properties are a great way to beat inflation and preserve your wealth and buying power. Because you lose 3% of your capital due to inflation each year, you have no choice but to invest, and real estate is a great starting point. For an investment property, aim for a minimum 3%–5% annual yield after all expenses. Buy and hold. Dot not flip, as this can be very risky.

Stocks are much more volatile than real estate, so be ready to hold for at least seven to ten years, and you will probably experience a big downturn or two during that time. Do not get emotional and sell at or near the bottom. Buying and holding is the best and safest strategy for any investment model.

Be very careful with fad investments like cryptocurrency. It's not for the faint of heart. You must be able to withstand 50% decreases in valuation and ride out the bad times. It's very volatile and can be an emotional roller coaster. Again, the strategy here is to buy and hold.

Lastly, be wary of your bankers who may try to sell you mutual funds or similar investment vehicles. Mutual funds come with standard rate fees such as 2% on the whole invested amount. That can eat significantly into your profits over the long term. On average, a 2% mutual fund fee works out to over 50% total fees in a ten-plus-year timeframe. So stay far away from these investment types.

at the mercy of any email, tweet, post, and call, and I would forget what I was supposed to do. I have had to get used to saying no. When you run your own business, friends and family may not understand. But don't be afraid to be selfish. Every time you say 'yes' to someone else and 'no' to yourself, you are giving away your hours. Prioritize your business. When you're your own boss, it is your livelihood.

PATIENCE

Results don't come in evenly. At the beginning, during your first few months of business, success happens slowly. The effort you put in will outweigh results. But then, as things in your business start aligning, because of your focus and persistence, your success will explode, and results will come in much faster than the effort you put in.

There are a lot of theories about what makes someone successful. Is it IQ? Well a lot of high IQ people end up underperforming and being marginal members of society. In the late 1960s and early 1970s, Walter Mischel, a psychologist and professor at Stanford University, conducted a test involving children and marshmallows to study delayed gratification and whether that could predict how successful they would be as adults. The test was simple. They asked kids "Do you want a marshmallow now? Or do you want two marshmallows two hours from now?"

Kids who wanted the marshmallow immediately tended to be the ones who preferred taking shortcuts and disliked working hard. Kids who could wait two hours to get two marshmallows, understood the value of holding out to get more. They tracked the progress of these kids for decades, and found that the kids who waited for two marshmallows did indeed become more successful as adults. They had a higher income, higher statuses, and a lower divorce rate.

THE ENTREPRENEUR
ROLLER COASTER

Failure is part of taking risks, and learning from mistakes is part of being an entrepreneur. We only have one life, so aren't you curious to know how far you can take it? If you're happy the way you are, don't change. Happiness is hard to come by. But if you're seeking a change and feeling unhappy, it might be because you're overwhelmed by negative emotions. Keep in mind, that EVERYONE experiences this at one time or another. I, personally, struggle with these feelings myself sometimes. It's impossible to eradicate them completely. What's important is how you manage yourself when you feel them.

It takes a lifetime to become a pro at controlling your mental state. Many of these emotions have served us well and protected us in the past, so our brains don't want to change. But we must recognize when they're helpful and when they're not, and make sure we aren't being reactive or illogical when we make decisions. So here are the biggest hurdles that all entrepreneurs struggle with and the solutions to overcome them.

FEAR

Fear was useful when we were cavemen, and were being chased by animals or fighting wars. In the present day, life is not that scary anymore. We have fight or flight instincts programmed into our minds, but this programming is out-dated. In 2018, what are we so afraid of? When I speak to entrepreneurs, their biggest fear is of the unknown. Fear of failure, fear of embarrassment, fear of pain. Once you figure out exactly what you're afraid of, you can build confidence to overcome it. Understanding fear is the key to defeating it. Fear is just our instinctual reaction to avoiding pain. The three types of pain that entrepreneurs face are loss pain, change pain, and outcome pain.

Loss pain is the fear of losing something. The biggest losses include losing your job, your house, your kids, your money, your security, your career path, your coworkers, and your food. It's the thought process that starts with, "What if...?" "What if something terrible happens if I do this?" This fear leads to worry about the things you can't control. But worrying about this is fruitless. Focus on what you can control.

One of my fiancée's biggest fears was not having job security. She is an example of an entrepreneur who didn't start off as one. She believed that her job gave her stability. But as she watched her coworkers get fired when her company restructured, and she struggled to get a promotion, I finally convinced her that her skills would be put to better use if she worked for herself in Ecommerce. Since then, she's been able to manage her own time and design our dream home. And she'll never have to worry about promotions or getting fired again.

My students' biggest fear is losing money. It's completely understandable. You worked hard for it. But you won't be able to be an entrepreneur if you have this mindset. You need to invest in your business and yourself. A restaurant owner will have to invest in the location, the equipment, the furniture, the staff, and the food.

A real estate agent will have to invest in their website, branding, photography, and advertising. These days, with online marketing, the barriers to entry and the financial risks are FAR less than they would have been in the past. So if you're scared of losing five dollars, you need to work on your entrepreneurial mindset. Keep in mind that entrepreneurial life has many more highs and lows than a 9 to 5 life. My biggest fear is not being able to afford the life I want, and not fulfilling my potential. My fear is a bit different because it pushes me to succeed, instead of paralyzing me with anxiety.

I think of the freedom, the exciting challenges, and the growth I'm going to experience by investing in myself. To me, the biggest risk is to live life without taking any chances. I know how the 9 to 5 life turns out. I've seen it all around me. I've decided that it isn't what I want, and the fear of living a mediocre life scares me more than anything.

The solution to fighting your loss pain is to think of all the things you're going to gain. Don't think of what you 'might' lose. Switch it around and think of what you might gain.

Change pain is the process of change. Changing is hard. Most of us are creatures of habit. We like to do things in a particular way, and we get stuck in our routines. The idea of doing something new is scary. It's unpredictable and makes you feel vulnerable. Most people do everything they can to avoid change. But change is part of our lives. Jobs get lost. Wages get cut. Rent increases. Food gets more expensive. You can't stick your head in the sand and hope that change won't affect you. Better to face change and be proactive instead of reactive. Better to choose how to change your life instead of having your life changed for you. Growth doesn't happen in a bubble. The solution would be to see change and challenges as a good thing. It's a way to push yourself and reach your true potential: to be your best self and have variety in life.

When my fiancée and I moved from Toronto to Kelowna, it was very difficult. We left our friends and our city lifestyle. Why did we do this? We knew that, for us, the city was a distraction. All we needed was our laptops and an internet connection for our business, and we understood how important environment was to our success. Being able to focus meant not spending thirty minutes looking for parking, not being stuck in traffic for hours, not being kept awake by people partying on the city streets, and not being distracted to spend money at the countless bars and restaurants. Since our move, our yearly income skyrocketed from six figures to seven. The change helped us grow, but we wouldn't have known this had we not taken the risk. What are you willing to change to reach your goals?

Outcome pain is the fear of a bad outcome. The biggest fear entrepreneurs face is failure. What if, after all the effort you put into your business, you fail? What if the grass isn't greener on the other side and your life isn't any better? First, be comforted to know that everyone fails. Failure is not a reflection of your character; it's what you do afterwards that counts. How do you turn it into something positive? I have failed many times, and it's not big a deal because I learn from it each time. In Ecommerce, we would launch thirty products a week and only one would be a winner. We'd launch one hundred ads per day and only thirty would work. The more you put yourself out there, the more chances you have of finding something that works.

Focus on positive outcomes, not negative ones. Remember, for every failure you face and learn from, there are other people who already gave up. Every time you push past your fear, your probability of success increases as the competition decreases.

FRUSTRATION & ANGER

When you start your Ecommerce business, one emotion that you will come across is frustration. You will feel frustrated if you aren't reaching the income you want and, if left unchecked, frustration can turn into anger.

Examples of unhealthy, unhelpful frustrated thoughts include:

- Why does everything go wrong for me?
- What does everyone else know that I don't?
- I'm failing because of someone else.
- I'm not being told all the information.
- I'm being tricked.
- My situation isn't fair.
- It's not my fault.
- This is impossible.

People who complain or make excuses rarely take action. When you're complaining, you are spending time and energy explaining why things are unfair and why you can't do it, instead of figuring out a solution to the problem.

In your Ecommerce business, you will work with other people. You will have staff, vendors, mentors, and fellow entrepreneurs. If you find yourself struggling, you might start looking for a cause. It's a quick downward spiral into blame or hopelessness. It's easier to blame a person or an unfair situation rather than to try and look for a solution. But if you allow yourself to become angry, it's hard to escape, and you might find yourself living there. Take responsibility for your business. When you're your own boss, the person held responsible is you. When something goes wrong, you must fix it. Look inside yourself for solutions and man up. Don't blame others for your shortcomings, and don't play the victim. Identify the problem and figure out what you can do to improve the situation.

Entrepreneurs must also be very careful about how they spend their time and energy. When running a business, we think in terms of ROI. What's the ROI of getting angry? Of proving your point? Of putting someone down?

Hold yourself to a higher standard. Learn to let things go and calm down. Anger is often a distraction. Keep the bigger picture in mind and pick your battles. Anger tends to make a hard situation worse. It could cause you to do things you might regret. Look for solutions, not problems. Remember the goal: your success.

LAZINESS

Laziness leads to excuses, distraction, and procrastination. It's a sign of an undisciplined and uncontrolled mind. These are the most common excuses I've heard:

- I'm too tired.
- I just don't want to.
- I'll do it tomorrow.
- It's too hard.
- I can't concentrate.
- I'm too busy.
- I'll do it when I feel like it.

Laziness comes from a lack of routine and discipline. As an entrepreneur, you are the boss. You must manage your workday and hold yourself accountable. Many people think that being an entrepreneur and having financial freedom starts from day one. That isn't going to happen for you until you have a steady stream of income, and have outsourced most of your daily tasks. Creating the bones of your business takes work ethic. What you must do to become a successful Ecommerce entrepreneur is think, type, and click. For those of you making excuses, life is not that hard. We have so many opportunities for making money, and modern technology means that we have more time to concentrate on improving ourselves.

Nowadays, even the laziest person can be an online success. You don't even have to leave the couch, if you don't want to. There are two types of laziness: long-term and short-term.

Long-term laziness is a much bigger problem for people than short-term laziness. You must decide if being lazy is hurting your business. Every day we lose time. If you have a life purpose, and you aren't accomplishing it, you might have long-term laziness. Long-term laziness is when you start to underachieve. It affects your daily routine and quality of life. If you're living at home with your parents and you can't get a job, you may be suffering from long-term laziness.

It doesn't have to look like sitting on a couch and getting fat. It can look like someone who is busy, but accomplishing very little. In this scenario, they are suffering from being mentally lazy, not physically lazy. This type of laziness can include the inability to make decisions, or procrastinating by browsing and overloading on information. It's simply a general inability to complete necessary tasks.

Short-term laziness is when the lazy feeling doesn't last as long and typically doesn't negatively affect your business. Maybe you don't feel like launching your ads for your Ecommerce store today, but you have staff trained to do it. Maybe you want to sleep in or answer your emails tomorrow. If there are no severe delays or consequences to your short-term laziness, this is perfectly acceptable, and all entrepreneurs have lazy days.

Successful entrepreneurs can experience laziness from overachieving. The drive that was there simply isn't there anymore, because life has become too comfortable. They lose their drive and their hunger, because they've already made it. This is when your motivation to avoid laziness must come from within. There are two sources of motivation: Inside and outside.

Figure out whether your motivation comes from outside or inside yourself. If you get motivation from outside, it's much easier to be lazy. If someone is telling you to do your homework, or telling you to eat healthy, but you don't really want to and it's not something you believe in, you will find it very hard to do.

People who are motivated from the inside have purpose and are less likely to be lazy. They have things they want to achieve. By sitting around watching television or sleeping all day, they aren't getting anything done. They feel pressure from within, to get up, and just do it.

While having external pressures or desires, like earning a lot of money, does manage to motivate many entrepreneurs to be successful, it's more long-term and effective to be motivated by something you believe in. Some people use negative emotion to motivate them. There are a lot of successful people who get very far with this. While it can be useful to drive you at the beginning, it's not long lasting or healthy. For example, if you want to lose weight, but your motivation is to look thin for your wedding, but not because you want to improve your physical health, you will probably put back all the weight after the wedding. It's not sustainable to be motivated by negative emotions. That's why the mindset and motivation behind the action is so important.

When I was in debt, I was faced with a choice: figure out a way to get rid of it or go bankrupt. This pushed me to fight harder because the fear of facing bankruptcy motivated me. But since then, I've had to find other ways of motivating myself; like leaving behind a legacy, helping others succeed, and building our dream home for our family. I also have goals to get financial education into schools, because I was led astray by credit cards and debt at such a young age, like so many others.

IMPATIENCE

Cultivating patience takes a lifetime to achieve, especially because the world is designed to teach us to want and expect instant gratification. So, what do I mean by being impatient? It's the idea that you can't wait to achieve your goals. Instead of focusing on the day-to-day, you're focusing on the result. This way of thinking is not going to work for the entrepreneur, because owning your own business does not mean you get to shortcut your way to success. How many times have you started a project and realized that it was much harder than you thought and gave up because it was taking too long? This is not how progress works.

It's much easier to look backwards than it is to look forward. When I look back, I am so grateful that we stayed patient, worked hard, and pushed through our boundaries. At the time, we didn't have many role models to follow in Ecommerce, and most of what we carved out for ourselves was brand new in the marketplace. But compared to just five years ago, our lives are completely different.

Tony Robbins says that we overestimate what we can achieve in a year and underestimate what we can achieve in five years. If you want results right away but you're not prepared to build on your knowledge and experience, you are limiting yourself. Think of your friends. I'm sure you have at least one friend who seems to constantly have a new project in the works, but never seems to finish any of them. Maybe that's you. They're so impatient to get to the goal that, when it doesn't happen immediately, they lose interest. This person will forever be starting from square one.

As an Ecommerce entrepreneur, understand that building a business takes time and staying power. Your brain is constantly looking for the next high. The next dopamine rush. Learn to ignore it and retrain your brain to focus. Impatience can also lead to mistakes, or taking risks for the sake of getting faster results. This is counterintuitive, as it can set your progress back by years. Be smart about your decisions and enjoy the journey. Don't miss what's in front of you. Focus on the results you have achieved, and appreciate how far you've come. It's a careful balance between ambition and gratitude. That balance is patience.

SELF-DOUBT AND SELF-HATE

Sometimes, when you're feeling frustrated and not getting the results you want, you start attacking yourself and your character. You will have bad days, but allow yourself a time limit for how long you're going to let yourself stay there. Life is too short to feel like crap. When you're the type of person who tends to blame themselves, you can really hurt your confidence. When you're an entrepreneur, there's a lot of pressure to succeed. Starting a new business is always going to result in hiccups. You need to learn how to deal with failure. Expect it, inspect it, learn from it, and carry on. Pick yourself back up and move forward.

If you're suffering from self-doubt, you might experience some of these negative thoughts:

- Maybe this business idea isn't a good idea.
- I don't think I have enough money to do this.
- I'm not smart enough to get this done.
- This doesn't seem like it's the right time.
- This is not going to work.
- I didn't really want to do this anyway.

Once you start doubting yourself, things can start to get out of control. It's really hard to get out of a negative thought spiral. You then might start to experience self-hate.

- Why is my business idea not working?
- Why aren't I smarter?
- Why can everyone else do it, but I can't?
- Why can't I do anything right?
- What's wrong with me?
- Why am I such a failure?

These thoughts can be crippling. The way your brain functions, is that it builds from past experiences. So maybe someone has said something negative to you in your past, and it's been making you doubt yourself. The solution is to understand the difference between your thoughts and reality. What you think is not necessarily the truth.

The first step to changing your mental state is to change your physical state. Exercise and get a dopamine boost. Then, focus on what you can control and what you can improve. Filter out negativity. If there's someone or something contributing to your self-doubt, remove it or remove yourself. Anybody would break down if they were bombarded with negative energy. Control your environment, and make sure that it is positive and helpful. If you're feeling doubt, reassess why you're building an Ecommerce business in the first place. Why do you believe it's so important? Re-evaluate what you're doing and find greater meaning in it. Make it imperative that you must succeed. Train your mind to think bigger than yourself and your self-doubts.

THE PERSONALITY
TRAITS OF SUCCESS

I n contrast to the last chapter, the following are some personality traits that I've found helpful for success as an entrepreneur.

FOCUS

You've quit your 9 to 5, so now what? There's no routine for you, unless you set it. There will be distractions everywhere, unless you remove them. Your business will have no focus, unless you stick to it. You'll be tempted to socialize, to spend hours on forums and newsfeeds, reading and commenting on posts. A lot of people think that socializing with other successful Ecommerce entrepreneurs is productive, but you're just chatting. Stop browsing. It wipes out your focus. Be careful of social media, because everyone will be fighting for your attention. Decide where you want to concentrate your attention, and do not get addicted to looking at everything and focusing on nothing.

Make a to-do list. Every morning, I write down my daily tasks and goals. I need my activities to have an intention, otherwise I would get distracted and my productivity would drop. I would be

They understood delaying gratification for a bigger payoff and a better future.

So can this be taught? This personality trait is something you are born with, but it can be learned. If you can grasp the idea that taking shortcuts does not get you better results, you can appreciate discipline and hard work. People are different from animals because we understand time. We can imagine the future. We have the ability to plan for tomorrow. It's a sign of intelligence when we can map out our futures. When we daydream, we are simulating worlds that don't exist.

When we make a plan, and wait for those two marshmallows tomorrow instead of one marshmallow today, we lay out the foundation for a more successful future. Ecommerce has the ability to pay out millions of marshmallows. The dedicated entrepreneur will take the time to design an optimized website and source hot products. Because this is not a get-rich-quick scheme, you will be working for tomorrow, not today. People who try to shortcut and do not have any patience will not find long-term success in this industry.

HUMILITY

Being humble allows you to stay curious, to learn, and to grow. You don't know everything. If you're too sure of yourself, you will start blocking out opinions that differ from yours, and you will stop growing. That's the death of an entrepreneur. If you've decided that there is nothing more anyone can teach you, you have essentially decided that you are done learning and growing.

The industry of Ecommerce is fluid and constantly evolving. There is always another way or even a better way of doing something. Be open to other strategies and consider your competition. What are they doing? Are they doing anything better? Do they have a better campaign, offer, or branding technique? Look outside yourself and you will improve. Even as a mentor, I'm constantly learning and evolving. This is a small industry. It's better to help each other than try to screw each other over. What may work for our business today may not work tomorrow. In Ecommerce, it is wise to surround yourself with people who run their businesses in different ways. There is more than one road to achievement.

ENVIRONMENT SCAN AND REVERSE ENGINEER

In our years of entrepreneurship, the best way to learn and take action is by doing an environment scan and reverse engineering.

What's an environment scan?
- Read lots and read often. Watch webinars and tutorials. Don't assume you know everything.
- Explore the Ecommerce landscape. What's working? What isn't? Join forums and Facebook groups, and find an Ecommerce mentor.

What does it mean to reverse engineer?
- Look at the people who've succeeded in areas that you also want to succeed in and do what they do.
- Find someone who has done something similar to what you want to do and reverse engineer the steps they took to get there.

When we decided to build our house, we didn't just sit and try to figure it out with our current knowledge. We did an environment scan. We asked other people who had built houses how their process worked, what they would do differently after going through that process, what they would warn us to avoid. Don't underestimate the power of the collective experience. Someone out there has gone through what you've been through and can inform your experience, making it better and easier. Do not reinvent the wheel. Starting from square one is much harder than improving a system that's already working and exists.

GROWTH

If you want to grow, you must do things that scare you and get you out of your comfort zone. You might think that staying comfortable keeps you happy, but if your dream life requires that you try something new, then that's what you're going to have to do. You'll feel like you're taking a risk, and you won't want to do it. You'll feel resistance. Your fear, your laziness, and your self-preservation will go into overdrive as you try to avoid pain.

When you go to the gym, the only way to build up muscle is to lift weights. If they aren't heavy enough or don't provide enough resistance, your muscles won't grow. It's no different with your mind. Resistance is your mind growing. It's what happens when something is challenging. Some people seek this out. When they see themselves being challenged, they push harder. I say that it's better to choose the challenges that you want to face, otherwise you'll just be facing the challenges that life puts in front of you.

People who have a growth mindset believe that abilities can be developed. They are the ones who say, "I love a challenge!" versus those who hate it. It's your approach to difficulty. The growth mindset sees challenges as "not yet" instead of failure. Just because you don't reach the results you wanted immediately doesn't mean you won't get there.

Those with a fixed mindset tend to run away from difficulty and will often try to compare themselves to people doing worse than they are to make themselves feel better. They might look for ways to shortcut their path to success, even if it means cheating someone.

The problem with modern education is that it fixates more on getting A's. Our report cards program us to want constant validation and, if we don't get it, we feel disappointed and discouraged. We need to praise the process more than the result.

Don't get me wrong, the result is very important too; but if we don't have a positive outlook on the process, we will never get to the result. Focus on growing in the right direction, and be confident that you will get there. Your attitude to problem solving will increase your likelihood of success. Stepping out of your comfort zone won't feel as big of a deal anymore, and you will focus more on growth, rather than your fear of failing.

GRIT

I use this term a lot when preparing my students for their entrepreneurial journeys.

This is a term coined by Angela Duckworth in her book *Grit*. It's what she believes is the key to success and achievement. She noticed that the smartest kids in her class did not do as well as the hardest-working kids. She realized there was something more important than IQ. It was effort.

Her research focused on what made someone successful and what didn't. She found that what predicted success was grit. Grit is the ability to achieve long-term success. It's knowing what you want, and being able to work toward it for a long time. This doesn't mean just doing what you like; it's being able to do things that you don't like as well. You are able to push through obstacles even if they're hard or boring. Do you have the ability to see past the present moment even through struggle and sacrifice? It's that hunger inside. The passion and perseverance to never give up. The stubbornness that says, "I will succeed no matter what."

So how do you get grit? Get clarity about what you want and

work toward that each day. Find meaning in it and make sure it's important to you. Be enthusiastic and optimistic, and believe in yourself. Surround yourself with people who aren't going to let you quit. Gym trainers make you give them 20 more reps when you think you've got nothing left to give. They push you harder than you think you can go. Remember that kid I mentioned who didn't sleep throughout my three-day event and made $80K revenue on the fifth day? Do you have that type of dedication?

LEADERSHIP

You might think that running your own online business will mean that you don't have to work with anyone ever again. But no Ecommerce entrepreneur gets successful all on their own. You're just one person. You need the humility to know that you can't do it all by yourself, and that you aren't the best at everything. Learn how to put together a great team to support you. A business shouldn't stop producing or working, just because you do.

To build a successful team, you need to look at everyone's attitude and enthusiasm. Skills can be taught, but it's harder to teach attitude. You're now the leader. This doesn't mean yelling or threatening to get work done. It means getting in the trenches and teaching by example. Don't act elitist, condescending, or threatening. Figure out the strengths and weaknesses of each team member, and work out how they can excel. Your staff may have great ideas on how to improve the business. Create an environment of open communication, and empower them to, not just follow orders but, to think for themselves. Get them invested in the business' success by incentivizing them with bonuses or rewards. Remember what it was like to have a boss. Be the boss you would have wanted.

THE MOTIVATED MIND

Staying motivated is one of the biggest challenges of being an entrepreneur. You need to be your own biggest fan, and remember the reasons why you want to lead an entrepreneurial life. No one will tell you to launch ads or products. You must be the one to direct your daily actions.

For my fiancée and me, our biggest driver and motivator was freedom. We wanted full control over our lives, and to be able to design what we wanted our days to look like. It's the reason we chose Ecommerce. We wanted the low start-up costs, the minimal equipment needed, and the flexibility of where we could work. We wanted to work hard, but smart.

With such a low barrier to entry, why do some people still lose their motivation? Why does it seem like some people have more energy, more focus, and more drive? Do you sometimes wake up and feel like you have so much drive and enthusiasm but other days you can't get off the couch? If you are finding it hard to motivate yourself to achieve your ambitions, you might have to consider that you don't care enough about your goal. We all have off days, days you don't want to do anything but sleep, eat, and hang out with friends. But if it becomes a lifestyle, then you aren't going to be putting in the hours or focus you need to succeed. You need to direct your actions toward your goal every single day. Every morning, visualize what you want your life to look like. But don't JUST imagine the end product; envision yourself doing what you need to do today to be able to get to your destination.

Starting a store can seem overwhelming. So break it up into little pieces. The best way to reach a destination is to lay out a roadmap. You might find yourself wanting to quit or say that your goal isn't important anymore. So planning helps you put your goal in front of yourself on a daily basis, and reminds you what you need to do.

Each morning, I write out a list of things I need to do on a piece of paper. Every time I complete a task, I cross it off. The act of crossing off something I've completed makes me feel satisfied about my progress. My brain can only hold about three things at one time. Writing my to-do list helps me concentrate on the task at hand, and gives me something to refer to when I need to know what to do next.

Beside my desk, I also have a whiteboard. I use this to brain-storm ideas. I just write every idea I have, in no particular order, just so I can visualize it. I then draw over it and reorganize it in a way that makes sense to me. The board is my big picture, and it provides me with daily direction and focus. And the to-do list breaks down my steps toward it.

While it's important to be disciplined and work hard, people can also lose motivation if they burn out. That's why you need to celebrate wins. Getting to your goal can't be the only time you let yourself feel achievement. That's why I like making lists and cross-ing off tasks that I've completed. I feel good about myself. Each task I complete is a win. Give yourself credit for achieving the small steps that you've planned for. Feel the progress and the gains. Feeling good about yourself makes you stronger and more confident.

At the end of every week, I take the time to reflect on what I've done, including the weekly wins. My fiancée and I practice self-care by going to nice restaurants or movies. Whatever makes you feel refreshed and ready for another workweek--do it. And truly share your wins. It will keep you positive, healthy, and motivated. Your attitude and enthusiasm will connect you to other people. It's good to feel proud of yourself.

When you join a community of like-minded Ecommerce entrepreneurs, they will keep you on your toes. It's inspiring to see other storeowners succeed. It encourages you to keep going, and that it is possible. Surround yourself with family and friends who will remind you of the goals you set. The ones who give you crap and nag you (in a nice way) about your workload. Stay away from those who discourage you or doubt you.

Inside our Facebook groups are top Ecommerce gurus and storeowners. We always compare notes and strategies and push each other in friendly competition. I make sure I surround myself with people who are much smarter than I am. I have a lot to learn, and there are a lot of people to learn from. If I'm in a room with people who are smarter than me, I am in the right place.

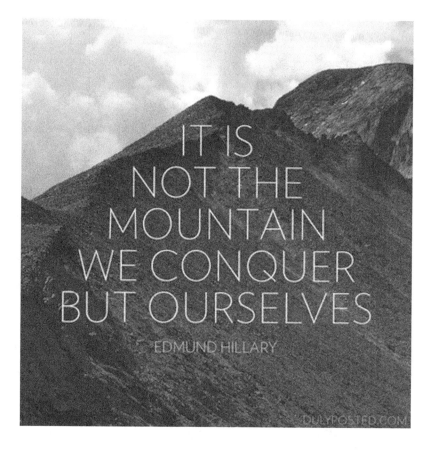

Source: dulyposted.com

THE PROBABILITY OF SUCCESS

L et's face it, many people fail. Most people don't know how to achieve their dreams, even though they have the potential. But here's the secret: it's a probability game. You need to break down aspects of your life that are hurting your success rate. So before you jump into launching an Ecommerce business, let's make sure your physical and social environment is conducive to being a successful entrepreneur.

One of the biggest factors affecting your ability to focus is your physical environment. If you have babies screaming in the background, or noisy neighbors, or friends begging you to come out to party, the odds are set against you. When I lived in Toronto, I felt like I had the mental knowledge and focus to be successful and everything lined up, except my physical environment. I lived in a condo right beside the CN Tower. People would run up and down the hallways screaming and yelling. Sometimes the fire alarm would go off in the middle of the night. I could hear the trams on the tracks and cars honking. When I wanted a break from work, I would leave my condo, get stuck in traffic, struggle to find a sixteen-dollar-per-hour parking lot, and line up to get into a noisy restaurant. This city was taking away a valuable asset: time. The time it took to get anywhere. The time it took for me to concentrate. The time it took from me getting a good night's sleep. Ecommerce allowed me to move anywhere. And I wanted everything in my life to line up for success. So I moved to a smaller town, and I haven't looked back since.

I live in Kelowna. There's no traffic here. No drunken noisy neighbours. Parking is everywhere and usually free. Life is just easier. When I want to relax, I actually relax. I can go to the golf course, or winery, or go on a boat. And this allows me to have the energy and focus to work. I might sound like I'm about ninety years old. I mean, don't I miss the city and all the action? Now and then I go back to the city, and it hasn't changed. The same parties are still there. Even the same people are there still partying. I haven't missed anything I haven't already experienced. Maybe a new restaurant or a new club? But I have the time and money to go there whenever I want. Don't get caught up in what everyone else is doing. It's a distraction from your own individual path. If you aren't seeing progress every five years and you're unhappy, have a look at your environment. People underestimate how much your location and lifestyle affect the quality and direction of your life and future.

Social environment is also integral to your success. If you have people in your life that are discouraging you or distracting you, your probability of success will decrease. Your social circle is probably stuck in a loop. Most people work 9 to 5 through the week and look forward to Friday. They spend their weekly earnings on the weekend, and must work to earn it back the next week. If you've been sharing your interest in becoming an Ecommerce entrepreneur with people who work 9 to 5, they won't understand what you're doing, and your goals will be completely different from theirs. Even parents don't understand. They are from a generation that believes you should just get a steady job and pay your bills, don't work on the weekends, and don't stress yourself out. Some friends and family will not understand your new lifestyle. You'll need to find new people who have similar life goals.

Your new social circle should include encouraging, like-minded, driven individuals. We're so lucky to live in the age of forums, Facebook groups and other online communities. Find other successful entrepreneurs. Attend webinars and events and join social groups. Feel the enthusiasm and optimism, and use it to fuel your business ventures.

THE LIFE OF ACTION

Many new entrepreneurs struggle with inaction. Inaction comes from the inability to make decisions. You may think that by doing nothing you are not making a decision, but inaction is a decision in itself. There is a lot of information out there on how to run an Ecommerce store, to the point where it can become overwhelming and paralyzing. You don't know which mentor or course to follow, or which action will lead to success or failure, so you don't do anything at all. But when you decide not to take action, you've decided not to be successful. Success does not come without action. An Ecommerce entrepreneur will have to make decisions every day. As your own boss, you will make the decisions to increase or decrease the budget, to hire or fire staff, to select products, margins, and many others.

Making a wrong decision shouldn't scare you as much as making no decision at all. Ecommerce moves fast. Ad strategies change all the time. Learn to make decisions faster and analyze the resulting data. Use the data to inform your decisions for the future. This doesn't mean taking action and making decisions without thinking. Check out the leaders in the industry. Observe your competition. Join a few forums and Facebook groups so that your information stays relevant.

The way that I found success in Ecommerce is by reverse engineering. I found mentors who were very successful and bought their courses. I looked at the people who had achieved what I wanted to achieve and followed in their footsteps. I didn't get overwhelmed with information gathering. I learned enough to be able to start testing myself, because there is no better or faster way to learn than by trial and error. It's about balancing thinking vs. doing. When you think without doing, you have paralysis by analysis. When you do without thinking, you'll end up being reactive instead of proactive. And at the end of the day, if you fail, you will have learned something valuable. Make informed decisions, use current knowledge, and take action. As long as you are progressing towards your goals every single day, your business will improve. It's simply a matter of time before you start getting successful. It takes hard work, dedication, and time. But, more important, consistent action. Try to accomplish one big thing per day that you can cross off your list. Whether it's launching your store, testing a new product, or firing up a new ad campaign, always take actions that help move the ball forward.

Wishing and hoping will never get you anywhere. Just reading this book won't either. You have to find the inspiration deep down, and grab the proverbial bull by the horns. Sheer will of action will make all the difference between growing or stalling your business. Don't underestimate the power of action. If you are working towards your goals daily, you will see improvement. And that improvement will feel good, pushing you to do even more. Never stop, never quit. If others can do it, so can you!

THE TICKING CLOCK

The biggest asset you have is time. Allocate your time in a thoughtful and productive way. Don't waste it on things you don't care about or haven't thought about. What's the ROI of time in your life?

One of the biggest regrets people face when they come to the end of their lives is that they didn't do more, and that they weren't braver. Time is more valuable than money. You can always earn money later, but you can't get more time. Even the richest billionaire can't live forever. Time is always ticking.

Spend your time learning things that will get you closer to your goals. Be selective with the knowledge you receive. Remove actions and distractions that don't add value to your life. Here's what I consider the biggest time wasters.

COMMUTING

People spend hours in their cars going to and from work. I know people who travel three hours to work and three hours back home. That's six hours! Five days a week adds up to thirty hours. That's one thousand, five hundred, and sixty hours per year.

INFORMATION OVERLOAD

This includes being on social media, Facebook, and Instagram, and looking at other people's lives or successes and wishing they were yours.

GOSSIPING/CHATTING

If you're networking with other entrepreneurs, make sure you're balancing it out with taking action, too. Don't get caught up in the trap of thinking you are being productive by chatting with others.

SHOPPING/BUYING/CONSUMING

You won't get wealthy lining someone else's pockets. Focus on selling, not buying. Save your profits, and invest for the future. Once you understand that you must sell to thrive, your whole world will change.

TELEVISION/MOVIES

I love watching TV and movies, but it's all in moderation. Don't be lazy and waste countless hours catching up or binge watching your favorite shows. They will be there forever. Focus on your dream, and work hard every day towards your goals.

VIDEO GAMES

I play maybe one hour per month max. Videos games can be highly addictive, so make sure you are not wasting precious time.

SCHOOL

University degrees and other conventional schooling can be a waste of time and money. There's no guarantee that all this money and time is going to result in a better paying job. A lot of degrees are completely unnecessary. School is not built for the individual. Their courses are formulaic, and may not be applicable to your future career. Nowadays, you can choose what you want to learn online, for far cheaper. This type of learning is a lot more useful, and usually taught by people who are living the life, instead of just teaching about it.

HELPING EVERYONE, BUT YOURSELF

You need to have boundaries. Helping everyone else, or taking on every project that comes your way, takes up valuable time. While it's great to be helpful, you are handing out your hours every time you say yes to other people. Make sure that by saying yes to someone else, you aren't saying no to yourself.

If you can gain two hours per day from things that aren't adding value to your life, and use them instead for something that will make your life better, that's 365 x 2 hours a day added to your year, a total of 730 hours! That's thousands of hours added to your life, decades of quality time. The biggest time ROI is investing in yourself, your family, and your business. Sacrifice now, for a better future. I'd rather sacrifice five years now, building my business every day, so that I can spend the next twenty years being more focused on my family, my happiness, and exploring the world. Most people don't retire until they're sixty-five and older. Do you really want to wait that long to enjoy your life?

THE BALANCED LIFE

No matter where you are on your Ecommerce journey, here are two things I'd like you to keep in the back of your mind: balance and happiness. Entrepreneurs have a habit of going 200% and forgetting about balance. While striving for your goals, you can often find yourself in a place of unhappiness. One part of your life might be running on empty. It's easy to forget that reaching your goals is only one part of happiness.

Don't be extreme. Aim to have a balanced life. When you start your business, you're going to want to go full tilt and give it everything you've got. This is expected and normal. But over time, you will seek balance. Just like riding a bike, you're not going to start off balanced. With practice, balance becomes easier. What does balance mean to you? It could mean:

- More time with your kids.
- More time at the dinner table.
- More dates.
- More sleep.
- More exercise.
- Better eating habits.

To me, balance has four main areas.

GOALS

Make sure that your goals are bigger than yourself and not just about making a lot of money. Find the unique purpose that drives you to take action.

EMOTIONS

Work on healthy relationships with family, friends, and even business partners. Do your kids, spouse or friends miss you? Make sure you spend enough time with them.

SPIRITUALITY

Have things you believe in. This doesn't necessarily mean a higher power. It could mean your ethics, and what you think gives meaning to your life.

PHYSICAL

Are you eating healthy and regularly? Do you have any bad habits, like drinking too much or not sleeping enough? Are you exercising?

Life can get overwhelming, but everyone has big demands, careers, and financial obligations. Some people protect their life balance more than others do, so if you feel like you've sacrificed too much of it, maybe it's time to get some back. And don't forget to enjoy the process. The secret to happiness is your attitude. Don't forget why you're striving for your goals. As we move through different chapters in our lives, our priorities change. Don't be afraid to reassess your original motivations, and make a shift if it's affecting your overall happiness.

Don't get overwhelmed. All the mindset changes may seem insurmountable, but the most important thing is that you start and you start *now*. Whenever you don't give up when something is hard, you're beating out all your competitors who *did* give up. Every time you push to the next level, your probability of success increases, because there are fewer people willing to work as hard as you.

You don't have to get all these skills mastered straight away. Just start building them at the same time as you build your business. Entrepreneurship is not about perfection. It's about striving to be a better you and leading a better life. Successful entrepreneurs are optimistic people. They believe in themselves, and they believe in their projects. There's enough negativity out there, and people are so skeptical, they would rather tear you down than fix their own lives.

Surround yourself with people who help you to reveal your best self, and don't lose sight of the ultimate goal: happiness.

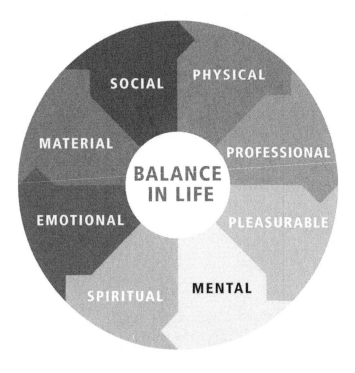

Source: pinterest.com

ACTION PROMPTS

1. Are you dead tired after work? How can you adjust your diet or exercise routine to find more energy in your day? What things are causing you the most tension in your life, and how can you release them?

2. What's taking up most of your energy throughout the day? Studying, playing video games, partying? What is killing your energy that you can sacrifice for the short term to get ahead?

3. Are you working yourself into the ground? Do you have sleepless nights wondering where your next income will come from? What can you do to focus your mind? Meditation, running, reading perhaps?

PHASE FOUR

THE ECOMMERCE LANDSCAPE

THE DEATH OF
BRICK-AND-MORTAR

The death of retail hit full swing in 2017. Brick-and-mortar stores who were supposed to be too big to fail, such as Payless Shoes, RadioShack and Toys 'R' Us, were among hundreds of retailers who filed for bankruptcy. What caused this retail apocalypse? Ecommerce of course. Mobile phone-driven shopping is exploding and making it easier than ever for people to shop from anywhere. At home, work, or a friend's house, wherever they have an internet connection, they can buy products.

Location-bloated mall chains and slow-to-evolve big box stores like Sears and Macy's were the main victims of the rise of Ecommerce. In the US alone, there were over 9,000 stores that shut down in 2017.

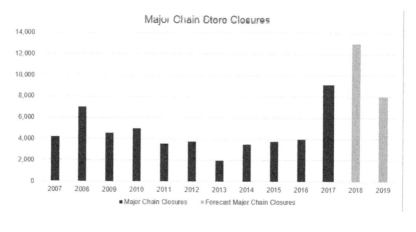

Source: Cushman & Wakefield

Here's a screenshot from one of my videos where I'm standing in front of a giant, abandoned Macy's store in Los Angeles:

11,000 stores will close this year, a 30% increase year-over-year. This is due to $70 billion in retail leasing that is expiring.

STORES CLOSING IN 2018

RETAILER	CLOSURES
Walgreens	600
Ascena Retail Group (Ann Taylor, Loft, Dress Barn)*	500
Payless*	408
Rue21**	396
Teavana	379
Gap Inc**	200
Toys R Us***	200
The Children's Place**	144
Vitamin World	124
Gymboree	102
Guess*	100
Charming Charlie	100
Crocs	64
Vera Bradley	50
Michael Kors	50
Kmart	45
Bon-Ton Stores	40
Sears	18
J.Crew	39
Macy's	30
Target	12
Last Call by Neiman Marcus	10

*Estimate based on company projections.
**Closures are currently in process.
***Toys R Us has not confirmed this number, which is based on news reports.

SOURCE: Company data   BUSINESS INSIDER

Source: Business Insider

This is the destructive power of Ecommerce. It is eradicating the old way of retail.

How many stores are going out of business because they're still relying on ancient marketing techniques like print ads in newspapers or relying on word of mouth?

People want convenience. They want to be able to shop from home and receive their order right on their doorstep within a few days. No one wants to deal with traffic, parking, or fight the crowds in an old run-down mall. Ecommerce is here to stay, and companies that don't make the shift online will be wiped out. It's only a matter of time before they go bankrupt or sell off.

How many stores, malls, and companies have you seen shutdown in recent years due to the overwhelming power of Ecommerce? No brick-and-mortar store is safe, because they simply can't compete on price, selection, or convenience. It's very frustrating these days to walk into a brick-and-mortar store and want an item that's not even in stock, will take two weeks to arrive, and require you to drive back to the store to retrieve it. That's bad customer service, in my opinion. Consumerism will never cease to exist, and it will only get easier for people to buy with the advent of new Ecommerce technology.

The cost of opening a physical retail location alone could be tens, or even hundreds, of thousands of dollars, and can put you in serious debt that may never be paid off if the business fails. But you don't have this risk when you launch an Ecommerce store. At most, your initial investment will be $5,000, and that's mainly for paid traffic and ad costs to start driving traffic and sales to your store.

The future is now. Don't be left behind. Jump on the Ecommerce bandwagon before it's too late. There's still plenty of profit to be made for the little guys like you and me. Amazon takes a considerable chunk of the total, but it's incredible what a small five- or ten-person team can accomplish in the first twelve months. I've seen people go from literally nothing to millions of dollars in revenue within six months. You and your customers will be eternally happier buying and selling online.

THE CURRENT STATE OF RETAIL

I t's never been easier to be an Ecommerce entrepreneur. With the internet at our fingertips, we can literally think, type, click, and make millions. Kids are doing it, grandparents are doing it, stay-at-home moms are doing it. There are so many platforms out there that make it easier and easier for us to create an online business. The barrier to entry is low. No longer do the big-box companies hold all the consumer attention. The internet has levelled the playing field, and now everyone can have a voice.

As we become more connected through social media, public perception and experience of a company is more important than ever. And, in the future, an Ecommerce store's branding will be an even higher priority than what it's selling.

You might think that what you are selling is more important than how you are selling it, but it's not. People need to identify psychologically with your company and its message. They are far more likely to buy from you if they feel good emotionally about the process. The way the smart brick-and-mortar stores are retaliating and keeping up with the online competition is by making shopping an 'experience.' They know that having an emotional and physical experience with a product is what makes them stand out from the crowd. I went into my local Best Buy and was surprised that they had rearranged their floor plans by brands instead of products. So instead of all brands being mixed together under Electronics, Home, and Entertainment, they had segmented into specific brands such as LG, Apple, and Microsoft. Each brand could rent out a space and display their products in the way they wanted the customer to experience them. This is also very smart for Best Buy because of the rent each brand pays for their space in the store. For example, Dolby used their rented space to set up a mini home theater that you could sit in.

So if brick-and-mortar stores know the power of branding and are switching up their displays to bond more with their customers, you can bet that online marketing will have to do the same. Consumers will buy based on their experience while buying rather than because of the products themselves.

THE BUILDING OF AN ASSET

The problem with platforms like Amazon, eBay, and Etsy, is that your traffic source relies on those specific communities, and you don't get the email list of buyers. When I sold t-shirts on Teespring, I didn't own the email list. I was building Teespring's email list, not my own. The benefit of owning your own store is that you own the email list. This email list is very valuable, because it's built up of subscribers and, most importantly, buyers. When you have an email list, you can email offers at zero cost. So all that money you spent, gaining leads and emails, can pay out at a very high ROI—if you have the email list. When you sell your store, the email list is a huge part of what makes your store valuable. If you have a list of 100,000 buyers, that will seem very attractive to the right investor. They know these customers have money, are online buyers, and which niche they are interested in.

On average, Ecommerce stores with good sales histories of at least twelve to eighteen months can fetch a selling price of 3X annual store profit. So if you made $1 million last year, you could potentially sell your store for $3 million. Talk about a big payday! And selling your store isn't as hard as you might think. There are numerous website brokerage firms who specialize is matching up buyers and sellers across the globe.

EmpireFlippers.com is a great example of a reputable website broker. They have an extensive buyers list of investors, who are actively searching for profitable and long-term Ecommerce stores to acquire. European and Asian investors are all the rage right now, as North American investors are pulling back investments from being too overstretched in the markets.

Build your store, grow it consistently month over month, and sell it down the road for multiple seven figures. Your store is truly an asset. Imagine what you would do after you liquidated a store. What would you invest those funds into next? Rental properties and stocks, I hope. As an entrepreneur, you must always be looking for opportunities, and Ecommerce gives you multiple ways to cash in.

If you want to get 5X–10X valuations, start up a subscription box company. Recurring revenue is worth a lot more to investors, because the income is so much more predictable. A simple example of this would be a "t-shirt of the month" program, where you would send an exclusive, member-only t-shirt for $19.95 per month. The best part of building a recurring business asset is that you don't start at zero each month trying to get more customers. You build and stack on your existing customer base that pays you month after month. This is why investors are willing to pay at much higher valuations than regular Ecommerce stores.

Combining physical products with a subscription program is incredibly powerful and ties well into building your brand. Customers will be excited for next month's offering, and churn will be low at price points between $10 to $40 per month. It provides an excellent upsell to your current customer base. So get out there and launch a recurring program of some sort to reap the benefits of more stabilized income.

The key to building and selling your business asset is all about timing. You don't want to try and sell your store when sales are down or in free fall. The best time to list and sell your store is when sales are booming, and each month's revenue is increasing. It's helpful to build a relationship with a website broker before you start scaling up a store, so that you have a solid plan for an exit. Niche stores are perfect for exiting in twelve to eighteen months because they are so focused on one type of product or niche. Keep some, sell some—it's all up to you!

THE GURU JUNGLE

What a difference two years makes! When I first started coaching, there weren't many Ecommerce mentors out there. Now it seems like everyone's grandma and their cat are calling themselves gurus.

These are the fly-by-nighters. Guru today, nobody tomorrow. These guys don't last. Be careful with the information you use for your business. Look for testimonials, screenshots, and professionalism, and someone who has been around for several years not just a few months.

This is the age where everyone is calling themselves an expert in their field. There are lots to choose from, so take your time.

It's a real guru jungle out there. Everyone's pitching their rags to riches saga. But don't get sucked into the sob story. It's nice entertainment, but what are their ad strategies? What are their methods for navigating the entrepreneur lifestyle?

You'll see a lot of ads with gurus standing in front of rented Lamborghinis and rented mansions. It's smoke and mirrors. What are they actually saying, and is it worth your time to listen? I've been told that it's a sad reflection of the quality of training out there, but students I've met have told me they are surprised that I seem to care about them so much. The ways in which people have been treated by so-called gurus has left them feeling burned. These guys don't care about your success. It's disheartening to hear the scams out there. It's bad for the industry.

These are the guys giving Ecommerce a bad name. We aren't scammers here. This is a real, legitimate, long-term business. Customers deserve a good experience when they are handing over their hard-earned cash. Don't let your desperation to make a quick buck distract you from becoming a business owner with integrity who is focused on the long term. I genuinely want you to succeed. I genuinely want Ecommerce to succeed. From a pragmatic point of view, it's in all of our best interests that we all succeed. Being an entrepreneur can be a lonely life, and you can't test for everything. Helping each other is the best way that we move forward and create a long-lasting business.

I truly believe that a rising tide lifts all boats. People have either a mindset of abundance or scarcity. Which one do you possess? Do you hoard and hide all your secrets and success to yourself, or do you share information with others, collaborate, and grow? So that's the kind of environment I've been building with my students. In our Facebook groups, we make sure to share, because we're all working towards the same goal, and we'll get there faster if we work together. It's incredible when you have such a dedicated group, open to sharing, with people who really want to help each other grow. The industry is morphing and evolving all the time; no one can hold all the keys. But, by collaboration, we can get enough data to understand the trends, peaks, and valleys as they appear in the Ecommerce landscape.

Now, I'm not saying that I am the right coach for you. Everyone learns and responds to information in different ways. I'm less interested in storytelling and more concerned with taking action. My students have consistently told me that I am a 'no fluff' style coach. So if you want someone who's going to be straight to the point and tell you how to run an Ecommerce business, I am the one for you. If you want a therapist, we will not be right for each other.

And not all gurus can teach. They may be able to get results for themselves, but are unable to replicate it for their students. I hear about the latest techniques other mentors come up with, and sometimes even I don't understand what they're talking about, because the language they use is so overly complicated. It's one thing to become successful on your own; it's a whole other thing to be able to teach others to become successful also. I've focused and prioritized teaching in simple, digestible chunks. We are not rocket scientists here. It's just an online store. I've had successful students under twenty and over seventy. Once you have the correct information, you'll be off to the races.

Ecommerce is built up of systems that are not complicated, but they do take time to set up. It's when the systems are set up and running on their own that you will experience that coveted entrepreneurial lifestyle.

In the next phase, I'll be teaching you the practicalities of setting up your Ecommerce business. I've broken everything down as much as possible and only included what you need. No fluff. My job is to simplify and not scare you off with too much information. So come on! Let's get to work.

ACTION PROMPTS

1. If you want to quit your day job, is Ecommerce the vehicle for you? Do you want uncapped income potential by building your own online store and selling worldwide to millions of people?

2. If you are studying full-time to join the workforce, analyze the Ecommerce opportunity and see if it makes sense. There are many young adults under the age of twenty-five who are crushing it online. Are you next?

3. If you already have an Ecommerce store, which guru email lists are you subscribed to? Which ones distract you from getting work done? Can you unsubscribe to some, if not all, so you can focus on growing your business instead of watching webinar after webinar?

THE ECOMMERCE BLUEPRINT

THE SIMPLEST
BUSINESS MODEL

The best business models are the ones that are easy to explain, are simple, and make sense.

The Ecommerce business model is just this.

1. Build an online store with an Ecommerce platform.
2. Have products in your store that are either physical or digital.
3. List your products online to people all over the world (using Facebook ads).
4. Make sales.
5. Send the products (fulfillment).
6. Profit and grow.

We will get into the details later in the book, but the idea is that, if you have something of value and show it to the right person, at the right time, and also have a platform where they can buy it and get it sent to them, you have a business. And that's Ecommerce in a nutshell.

THE TOOLS YOU NEED

Now that you've heard several reasons why Ecommerce is the answer for you, let's take some action and start with the tools you'll need to succeed.

US DOLLARS

Number one, it's best to keep everything in US dollars (USD). Why? Because 80% or more of your sales will most likely be from US customers. So you will be receiving funds in USD. You will also be paying for fulfillment in USD. And you will be paying for Facebook ads in USD.

This means you will need a USD bank account. If you are in a country where it's difficult to open one, you can look at Payoneer. com, which provides online accounts for this reason. Keeping everything in USD will allow you to avoid currency exchange fees, which can be anywhere from 2%–5% per transaction. This can seriously eat into your profitability.

US DOLLAR CREDIT CARD

Next, you will need a USD credit card with a high limit. The higher the limit, the easier it will be to run your business. Because cash flow is so crucial to making this business tick, you need enough room on your credit card to scale without having to pay it off daily just to keep up.

You can start with a low limit like $5,000, but once you really start to ramp up your business, having a $50,000 credit card limit is extremely helpful and will let you sleep easy at night knowing your ad account won't randomly stop spending on ads because you reached your limit.

A FACEBOOK AD ACCOUNT

In order to run ads and buy traffic, you need a Facebook ad account. Now there are two ways which you can create ad accounts. The first is from your personal Facebook profile. The second is from your Business Manager. Never use your personal Facebook ad account through your profile. Always create ad accounts using your Business Manager via https://business.facebook.com. Your BM, for short, is a place where you can create ad accounts, fan pages, and set up pixels, payments, and employees. If you were to create an ad account using your personal Facebook profile, your chances of getting banned or flagged from the platform increase greatly. Facebook heavily prefers Business Manager. And you can create two BMs per Facebook profile.

Now, each BM starts off with the ability to create at least one ad account. And after you warm up that ad account with enough ad spend, Facebook will allow you to create even more ad accounts. At first, you can create five more, then fifty more, then as many as eight hundred more. The more ad accounts the better. You want to have many back up accounts just in case they get banned for whatever reason. It's critical to have a backup BM always, just in case. This will limit your risk in case you start to scale your campaigns, and get shut down suddenly.

Source: facebook.com

AN ECOMMERCE PLATFORM

There are many Ecommerce platforms to choose from but, which-
ever you choose, the concepts within this book will still apply. I've
tried and tested the majority of them, and I found them to be inad-
equate for marketing. So I built my own.

Other platforms were built before Ecommerce took off, or features
were added as users needed them, through third party apps. There is no
platform built specifically for this business model. CommerceHQ is a
platform built for marketers, by marketers. It has all the apps you need
built right in, and all our themes are built for maximum conversion.
We also have a revolutionary Visual Builder that allows you to customize any of our built-in themes with drag-and-drop functionality.

After paying almost one thousand dollars per month for another platform that started at $29 (very misleading), we decided that we didn't want to create a platform like that. Instead we opted to charge one low fee per month, with everything you need to succeed right out of the box. No more paying extra for all those third-party apps that can slow down or even break your store. We are obsessed with conversion rate optimization and are always improving the platform each month to be faster, more powerful, and simpler to use than any other Ecommerce platform out there.

Imagine being able to get your store up and running within twenty-four hours or less. The record for a store setup so far is five minutes and nine seconds. Crazy fast. And if you aren't that 'techy,' then this is the platform for you. Our customer support team is second to none, and we will not rest until you are satisfied with the software, your store, and your business. We have a vested interest in your success and want you to achieve higher growth by working closely with our team. Try us out for fourteen days for free; you won't regret it: https://CommerceHQ.com. Here's a sample of the dashboard after you login.

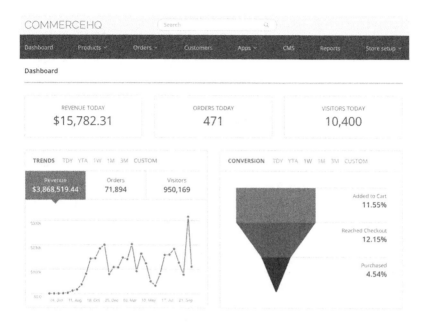

Okay, that's enough pitching. Thanks for checking it out and, hopefully, I will see you in the mastermind group soon!

A COMPANY

Regarding your business structure, you can typically run an Ecommerce store as either a sole proprietor or corporation. There are many tax benefits for running a corporation and, if you're American, you'll be using an LLC. Seek professional advice from your accountant or attorney on which structure makes the most sense for you.

At the start, you want to keep expenses low, keep profits high, and keep reinvesting in your business to grow it fast. Make sure you are set up to succeed with the right tools for the business. Accounting and taxes should be left to the professionals. Invest in your future and don't play the guessing game, because there's only two things certain in life: death and taxes.

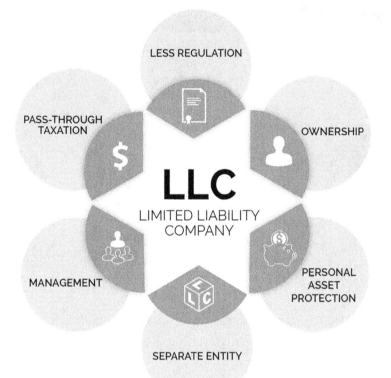

Source: howtostartanllc.com

THE BORING STUFF
YOU NEED TO KNOW

don't want to hear excuses. I hear you groaning and see you rolling your eyes. But if you want to own your business and call the shots, then it's time to 'adult.' It's not uncommon for business owners to want to ignore the boring stuff like finances, accounting, or law. You can hire these tasks out to professionals but, if you don't know the basics, you will get taken for a ride. I'm keeping this section short, because I'm not an expert. I sought advice from professionals who make a career out of helping entrepreneurs like me. Part of being successful is to know your limitations and to find the right people to help you. The following topics include accounting and law, which I failed at university. It came back to haunt me, because these are necessary life skills for any business owner.

A lot of what makes a business successful is risk mitigation. Whether you like it or not, the world has rules. Learn them and work with them, or else they have the power to make your life miserable.

FINANCES

Finances can be complicated, but if you can understand this simple concept, you will already be ahead of the game: **Your income must be more than your expenses.**

This should be your guiding star. Of course, at the beginning of a business there will be costs. But you can minimize and monitor those costs by keeping records, and not incurring expenses that you don't need. For example, when picking an Ecommerce platform, be aware that some platforms only give you a very basic template and charge you monthly for any additional apps or features. These extras can add up quickly. When you're just starting out, it's smarter to keep your expenses low and invest in paid traffic.

Don't be a collector of Ecommerce courses. Education is an investment in your development. But pick a mentor who you trust, and who has lots of testimonials from other students. Hold yourself accountable to take action. It's not actually an investment if you don't learn from the course.

Also, do not even think of starting a business if you have crippling debt. If you have a family that you're struggling to feed, or if you must refinance your house to invest in your business. Do not do that. The stress that it will put on you and your family will hinder your ability to make the right decisions for your success. Don't be a gambler. Get your life in order before you take risks.

ACCOUNTING

When I first started my business, I mixed all my funds together. Take it from someone who found out the hard way, you don't want to spend time untangling your finances, paying a ton of money to accountants, and having your attention taken away from what you do best—your Ecommerce business.

There are many strategies for reducing taxes that can save you tens of thousands of dollars per year. This is money that you can reinvest into your business. It took us three accountants to find the right one for us. Not many accountants are experienced in Ecommerce, so they will have a lot of questions about how your business works. It's worthwhile to do your due diligence and interview multiple professionals to make sure you are set up with the best possible business structure. Depending upon where you live in the world, you will have different options for setting up your business.

I can say, without a doubt, that finding a great accountant helped our business in a big way, and made it so much easier to sleep at night. You don't want to be waking up one day to a huge tax bill you didn't see coming. Do your homework, and set up your business the right way.

I'm still learning accounting strategies to minimize my taxes and I still need bookkeepers to organize my expenses. I'm definitely not an expert, but I know that avoiding accounting can slow your business down substantially.

LAW

Ecommerce is a relatively new industry, so you need expert advice on cross-border laws. Did you know that there are laws in the USA that require children's clothing to pass certain certifications before they can be sold to the public?

Take drawstrings, for example. Those are considered a hazard to young children, because they could strangle themselves. A fellow Ecommerce owner was selling baby moccasins by the boatload before he found out that the material in the moccasins did not pass US code. The fines are massive for selling these items unlawfully.

Hire a lawyer if you are scaling up and have doubts about the legality of your products.

INSURANCE

The best-case scenario to cover all your bases is to load up on insurance. Depending on your coverage and plan, this can include accidental copyright infringement Insurance and lawyers' fees. This is useful in case you create a product that infringes on someone's patent that you didn't even know existed, or if someone injures themselves from using one of your products. Accidents happen. Ecommerce is such a new industry. If you're earning upwards of seven figures and selling thousands of products per day, it's best to get insurance just so that you can sleep easy at night.

MATH

When I find a student of mine who can't do simple math, they're going to get an earful. And there's no excuse, because I failed math at school, and I can still run numbers. We aren't doing algebra or trigonometry here. It's basic addition, subtraction, multiplication, and division.

How do you expect to understand if your business is profitable if you can't even do simple arithmetic?

Calculating profits is math. Understanding margins is math. Every day, you will need to input numbers into a spreadsheet called a Return on Investment (ROI) sheet, and this is the Ecommerce entrepreneur's lifeline. These numbers give you transparency into what is going on in your business and what needs to be improved or changed. How can you expect to know how to optimize, or when to optimize, if you don't know your numbers?

I've had many students come to me not understanding how to correctly input their data into their ROI sheets. If this is where you struggle, I suggest you improve this skill before spending thousands of dollars on Facebook ads.

Please do not run your business blindfolded, crossing your fingers, and hoping for the best. It is so frustrating when I end up teaching math instead of helping someone scale their business and helping them profit. We're talking third grade math skills. And you can use a calculator or a spreadsheet to calculate everything automatically.

Understanding reporting and return on ad spend (ROAS) goals is another important aspect of running your own business. Know where your numbers need to be in order to profit. A lot of Ecommerce is about how you interpret the data from your clicks and sales. If you're getting a lot of sales but aren't profiting, you may need to raise prices. If you're getting a lot of add to carts, but no sales, you might need to lower your prices. You are buying data. Don't waste your money by not having basic math skills.

THE TERMINOLOGY
OF ECOMMERCE

M arketers often sound like they're speaking another language. Sometimes I forget that not everyone knows what ROI or LTV means. Listed below are terms that come up frequently in this book.

Over time, these terms will become second nature to you and, before you know it, you'll be fluent in the language of Ecommerce.

ROI = return on investment (calculated by taking net profit divided by ad spend)

ROAS = return on ad spend (calculated by taking revenue divided by ad spend)

CPM = cost per mille or thousand (how much it costs to show your ads to one thousand people)

CTR = click-through rate (the percentage of people who clicked on your ads)

CPC = cost per click (how much it costs when someone clicks on your ads)

ATC = add-to-cart (when a visitor clicks on your add-to-cart button)

CPA = cost per action, acquisition or purchase (how much it costs to get a conversion or sale)

AOV = average order value (how much on average people spend on your store per order)

LTV = lifetime value (how much on average people spend on your store over time)

ACTION PROMPTS

1. If you are a wage slave and are serious about Ecommerce, the time to start preparing is now. Save at least 10% of your paycheck towards your new business fund. Set up all the tools necessary *now* to get comfortable with the process.

2. If you are at college or university, start studying finance, accounting, and law. Then you will be equipped with the right knowledge when it comes time to launch your online store.

3. If you own a company, do you have a good accountant, lawyer, and banker? Are you set up to scale without worrying about small credit card limits? Do you have a good corporate structure to minimize taxes as much as possible?

PHASE SIX

THE BUILDING OF YOUR STORE

THE CREATION OF YOUR BRAND

You've made it! This is what you've been waiting for. It's time to start building your online store.

In this chapter, I'm going to focus primarily on branding, and how important it is to distinguish yourself from the competition. I'll take you through choosing your domain name, logo, colors, theme, font, and images. The identity and the look and feel of your store are incredibly important for your business success. You must have a clean, good-looking store that's easy to read, with professional images throughout.

You'd think that having the lowest product pricing in the market would get you the sale. But that's not always the case. Nowadays, the most important thing is branding. You could be more expensive than your competitors, and have less funding from investors, but if your branding is unique and you have a loyal following, you will have customers for life.

Branding is the best tool to create value, so that you can sell your company in the future for hundreds of thousands, or even millions, of dollars. You can command higher prices, have more repeat customers, convert traffic more easily, and hire more effectively when building your team. Now I don't expect you to go out and become the next Coca-Cola, Firefox, Google, or Amazon. You're probably never going get there unless you have millions to invest into branding campaigns. But you can get a lot of great ideas from these big brands.

What brand means today, is a person's gut feeling about a product, a service, or company: how someone truly feels about your business. Brand is what people say about you when you're not in the room; what they think about your business. It's the experience your customers have when they visit your store and buy your products. It's how you communicate with them. People mostly buy based on emotion not logic. So how do you trigger emotion that moves them? By having the right brand and setting up your store the right way, you can trigger emotions with your customers so they buy again and again.

You need to create a charismatic brand in three parts:

1. Have a brand mission or vision of where you are now and where you want to go.
2. Have a brand voice. Your copy will determine the impression you give to your customers. It's how you write your ads and product page descriptions.
3. Create an About Us page. Have a unique brand look. This includes how your store is designed: your color scheme, your logo, your fonts. Photography plays a big part in this. All these things are major factors of how your company is visually represented.

In this section, I'm going to tell you about the key components required to set up your online store. I will be taking you through the store set-up on CommerceHQ; so if you are using another platform, make sure you find the equivalent actions to take.

DOMAIN NAME

We'll start with your domain name, which is your website URL. If you don't have a professional domain name, people aren't going to take your store seriously. You're going to have a very hard time converting traffic into sales. If your domain name doesn't make sense with the products you are selling, or is too difficult to remember, it will be harder to sell the business down the road. I always recommend two to three word domains. Always use a .com domain. Never use .org, .net or any other domain name extension. Dot com is better for resale and adds trust and authority to your online store. Keep it simple and avoid dashes at all costs. Your website name needs to be easy to remember and easy to type.

Here are some examples of great words to use when coming up with a domain name:

- bargains
- best
- clever
- cool
- daily
- deals
- fast
- gadgets
- gold
- hype
- OMG
- passion
- pod
- pop
- shop

- stock
- store
- stuff
- super
- trending
- trendy
- true
- unique
- viral
- zen

You can mix these words with each other and try to find a domain that's available to buy for $10. Within your CommerceHQ dashboard/admin panel, you will be able to purchase domains and connect them to your store. In general settings, you should block search indexing on your subdomain, because this means that your competitors won't be able to find you on Google, so make sure that's switched on.

LOGO

Let's talk about logos. It's cringe worthy when people use Microsoft Paint or WordArt or ClipArt. It looks amateur, so please never try to make your own logo unless you're a graphic designer. Get a professional to create one for you. Your logo is the first thing that people really see when they enter your store, so it's important that it looks good. You can get an amazing logo done up at Fiverr.com, Upwork.com, or 99Designs.com. Here are some great examples:

Now you can see from these examples how easy these fonts are on the eyes. They mostly use a two-color scheme, max three colors. The logo could be cute, like the UpKiwi logo, or bold like the Trending logo. Emporium Pop has a more luxurious feel, very clean, and just one color—black. Putting a slogan under the logo, like TrendyShack does, is very smart. Freaky Pet has an original logo that's memorable. I'm going to be talking a lot about Freaky Pet, because they've done an incredible job branding their online store. It's probably the best example I can show you of branding.

COLORS

I want to take you through a kind of an interesting experience that happened back in the sixties with Procter & Gamble. They set up an experiment with three households and three ladies using laundry detergent. The first lady was given laundry detergent that was yellow in color, with little yellow specks in the detergent. She said that the detergent didn't quite clean her clothes well enough, and they were still very dirty. The second lady was given red laundry detergent, and she said that it damaged her clothes. The third lady was given blue detergent, and she said it was the best-smelling and best-cleaning detergent she'd ever used. Now this was an absolute breakthrough, because we didn't understand, as marketers, how color truly affected the mind in the buying process. Interestingly, green had the same effect as blue. If you look in the supermarket these days, you can see that most laundry detergents are blue or green in brand color. Sometimes they have a little red just to get your attention, but they are mostly blue or green, because that was proven to show higher conversion and satisfaction with laundry detergents. What an experiment!

So think of the emotions you want your customers to feel when looking at your website and logo colors. Make sure it's relevant to the product you're selling and keep it simple. Use two to three colors max. Below you will find a screenshot from Adobe Color, a great resource to find color themes that look great with your store.

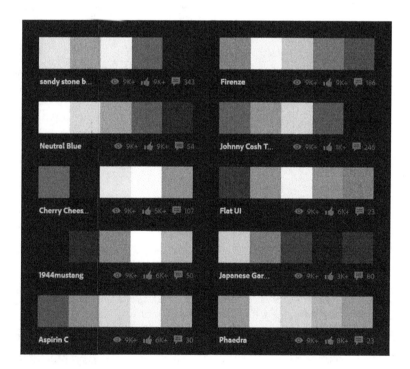

Source: adobe.com

THEMES

Your theme is the look and feel of your website. Themes have built-in site layout, navigation, fonts, colors, and more. Not all themes are created equal. Some themes may look pretty, but they may not convert well. There are key factors that help with higher conversion rates with your theme, such as large add to cart buttons, images, and titles. For example, with CommerceHQ, you get access to premium themes that are optimized to get you more sales and revenue. We have many themes to choose from. And the best part is you can customize them to your heart's content with our drag-and-drop Visual Builder.

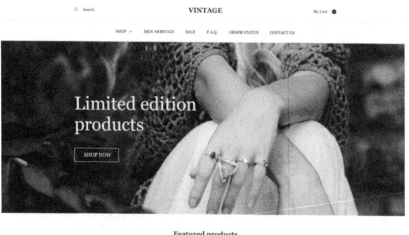

FONT

Fonts greatly contribute to the overall look and feel of your store. Imagine you're driving down the highway going eighty miles per hour, and you're trying to find your exit. Now if you see a sign like this, how hard would it be to read while driving? Obviously, very difficult.

That's why we build signs on highways like this instead:

Fonts must be easy to read at first glance, so that drivers can easily get the information they need. For your business, use fonts that are elegant and timeless. Most high-power Ecommerce stores use black-and-white fonts, which signify luxury. But there are other stores as well that are more colorful and more whimsical with their fonts, and it still looks great. The key is to make it look professional. Never use all caps, ever, other than for headings and buttons. The brain only sees rectangles, and it takes twice as long to process the information if it is in all caps.

Be careful with line length as well. Nine to twelve words max per line is ideal. You must be able to see the entire line at once. Also, don't have some things centered and other things left or right justified. You want to have everything in unison, so it looks clean and is easy to read. And be careful with line spacing. You only want to have 1.5 max spacing between lines. Do not use light text on a dark background, as people's eyes get tired using this scheme. That's why you see most Ecommerce stores with a white background. It looks better, it's easier on the eyes, and converts higher.

IMAGES/PHOTOGRAPHY

Now let's talk about photography. If you saw two different stores with the same product, which one would you buy from—the store with the product image on the left or the right?

It's almost the exact same image. They just rotated it, cleaned it up with Photoshop, and added a white background. Obviously the one on the right-hand side looks much more professional and trustworthy. That's the approach I want you to take when you're selecting images for your store. You can get great images from Shutterstock or other stock photo websites. Incorporating people into your images is also proven to increase conversion rate. A great example of this is someone using the product and showing it off using their hands. You can tell a story with images. You want to set the scene. Look at the example below.

This is the exact same photo as the one I'm going to show you next. But look at the difference. If you saw this on a store, you probably wouldn't think it's very trustworthy. But what if you saw this image on a store?

It's the same image, but it's cleaned up with Photoshop and looks so much more professional. That's the direction you want to go in terms of branding your store with photography. You want to make it look professional, crisp, clean, and easy on the eyes.

THE ANATOMY OF
YOUR WEBSITE

E very store website tends to be made up of the same essential sections. For example, headers and footers are the same on every page of your website. The header is where you add your logo and store name. Footers usually consist of navigation links and your store phone number.

You've got navigation that helps your customer explore the website. You'll need to link to the Home page, Product page, About Us page, FAQ, and Contact Us page. Then you'll need a Cart page and Checkout page, where customers can add products to their shopping cart and buy your products.

NAVIGATION

Start with navigation, so your customers can easily make their way around your website. Include these tabs: Home, Collections, Shop, About Us, FAQ, and Contact Us.

HOME   COLLECTIONS   SHOP   ABOUT US   FAQ   CONTACT US

HEADER AND FOOTER

Let's talk about header now. Here's a great example:

You have your logo on the left, search bar in the middle, and then on the right, you have your phone number, store hours and support email. Get a 1-800 number from Grasshopper.com, and record your voicemail, or get one professionally done at Fiverr.com. Put your phone number on every page or in the header and footer.

For the footer, you will need navigation for Terms, Privacy Policy, and Contact Us. Add credit card logos to establish trust and authority. You can include shipping information in the footer as well. An opt-in box works well to collect leads. But you definitely want to have your email, your phone number, and trust icons in the footer. Here's a great example:

You can make awesome footers like this using the Visual Builder on CommerceHQ. This is a very clean design that is pleasing to the eye and laid out well. They use a two-color theme here as well, which looks great.

HOME PAGE

Your Home page is your 'store front.' But unlike a brick-and-mortar store front, it's not always the first page your customers see. This is because, when we advertise products on Facebook, we always take the customer directly to the Product page, not the Home page. Ninety percent of your traffic is going to be landing on your Product pages. Although the Product page is the most important page, the Home page layout is where your store identity lives. So it's important to have a nice-looking Home page to establish your brand.

Design a nice big banner image related to the store name below the navigation links and logo. You can use stock photography or have it done professionally by a designer. Create a Bestseller Collection or Featured Products section below the banner image. Then make sure you have a promotional bar at the top of the page. The promo bar will say something like "Get free shipping when you spend more than $50."

Include a phone number of course, and you can get a 1-800 number from Grasshopper.com. Put that up in the top right corner of your store, or somewhere that's above the fold and visible on every single page, especially on the Home page. This adds a lot of trust and higher conversion rates as well. You can also have the store address and support email in the header/footer.

Fill up the Home page with a variety of elements, including images, banners, written content, and collections. It helps build trust when you have a full looking Home page that still looks crisp and clean, but is filled up.

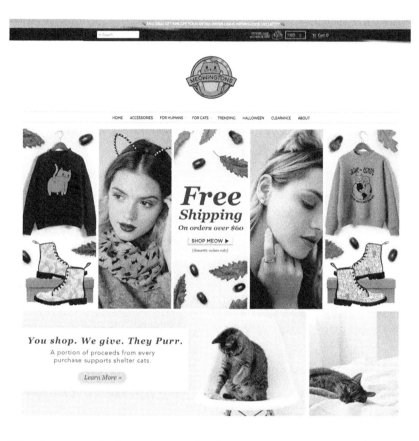

Now look at this clever banner hack:

Let's analyze what they did here. They have a photo collage of happy customers wearing or using their products. Wicked smart. Five stars as well—awesome. You could easily implement that with your own store or get images from AliExpress.com (more on this website later) from the reviews of the products that you're going to launch.

The next thing is trust elements. Trust elements are badges that let the user know that your site is safe to use. You want to plaster these all over your store. Example below:

You want to use these types of security badges, logos or trust elements to show that you're a reputable brand and that you're trustworthy. A good example here is "Worldwide Shipping, Secure Transactions, 30 Day Money Back Guarantee, Easy Returns."

COLLECTIONS PAGE

Under the tab "Shop" is where you'll have your categories of products. If you have a clothing store, you may have categories like Shirts, Skirts, Leggings, and Socks. You may choose to categorize by gender with collections like 'For Her' and 'For Him.' When your customer clicks on the collection, they will be directed to a collections page with all the products within that category. It's important that your product image and prices are all displayed clearly, with high resolution pictures and professional photography.

Collections

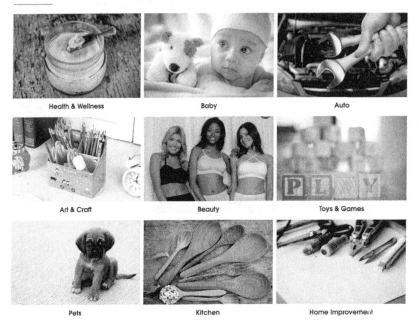

Health & Wellness	Baby	Auto
Art & Craft	Beauty	Toys & Games
Pets	Kitchen	Home Improvement

PRODUCT PAGE

Let's talk about your Product page. This is the most important page on your store because you'll be sending most of your traffic to the Product page from Facebook ads and other sources of traffic. You want to send all your customers to the Product page, because that's how you're going to make the most sales and have the highest conversion rate possible.

You'll need a nice, recognizable title, with an obvious and clear call to action, and a large 'add-to-cart' button. Place countdown timers and security badges, and include great photos of your products. Here's an example of a high-converting product page.

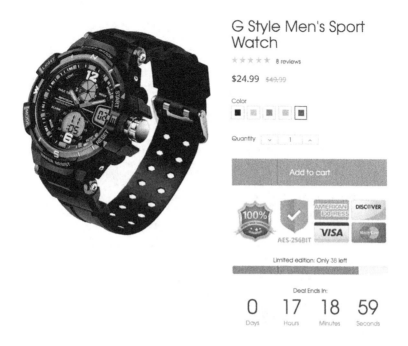

ABOUT US PAGE

The About Us page is your chance to share your story. Very few on-line stores have brand stories. You can go to Upwork.com and hire a copywriter to come up with a great brand story. Here's a perfect example of brand story from FreakyPet.com. It's on their Home page and their About Us page:

WHO THE HECK IS FREAKY PET?

Hey human! We knew you gonna land here because we know a lot about you and your love for us – cats and dogs. You, humans, are very curious creatures, so this is our story to learn.

Once upon a time, cat Zig and dog Zag were wandering through the beaches of Florida, not knowing each other. While each of them was leaving a separate zigzag trace in the sand, they had the same thought on their mind.

They both knew that people love cats and dogs equally and that it would be great to do something about it... something wonderful, a bit quirky and positively crazy, just like human love for pets is. But what could that be?! The same thought was driving them crazy!

However, the gods of all animals had a plan all along. A plan that was aligned and destined. Paths of Zig and Zag were about to cross. One shiny day both of them were wandering through one of Miami beaches thinking about their next move... and then it happened! The moment they saw each other from the distance they just knew it!

They recognized the crazy sparkle into each other's eyes and they knew they are going to do something extraordinary together. Since then, Zig and Zag, cat and dog, are joined with friendship and a common vision. After many long hours of brainstorming and miles of the double trace left on Florida's sandy beaches, their vision has embodied into Freaky Pet. They both agreed that without a dose of craziness there are no extraordinary things...and Freaky Pet was born.

Today, Freaky Pet is adding the crazy sparkle to the pet market, that makes cats and dogs owners jumping and freak out for joy. We offer a great range of custom made pet products, which are exciting, a bit quirky, a bit crazy – just alike the sincere love that human have for us as pets.

"Hey human! We knew you were gonna land here because we know a lot about you and your love for us—cats and dogs. You, humans, are very curious creatures, so this is our story to learn.

Once upon a time, cat Zig and dog Zag were wandering through the beaches of Florida, not knowing each other. While each of them was leaving a separate zigzag trace in the sand, they had the same thought on their mind.

They both knew that people love cats and dogs equally and that it would be great to do something about it… something wonderful, a bit quirky and positively crazy, just like human love for pets is. But what could that be?! The same thought was driving them crazy!

However, the gods of all animals had a plan all along. A plan that was aligned and destined. Paths of Zig and Zag were about to cross. One shiny day both of them were wandering through one of Miami's beaches thinking about their next move… and then it happened! The moment they saw each other from the distance they just knew it!

They recognized the crazy sparkle into each other's eyes and they knew they are going to do something extraordinary together. Since then, Zig and Zag, cat and dog, are joined with friendship and a common vision. After many long hours of brainstorming and miles of the double track left on Florida's sandy beaches, their vision has embodied into Freaky Pet. They both agreed that without a dose of craziness there are no extraordinary things…and Freaky Pet was born.

Today, Freaky Pet is adding the crazy sparkle to the pet market, that makes cats and dogs owners jumping and freak out for joy. We offer a great range of custom made pet products, which are exciting, a bit quirky, a bit crazy – just alike the sincere love that human have for us as pets."

I hope this example inspires you to get creative with your own brand story. If you aren't the creative writer type, like most of us, you can hire someone to write it for you. Story helps create the store experience and drive emotion in people to trust and buy from you.

CART AND CHECKOUT PAGE

Let's talk about the cart and checkout pages now. Most people really mess this up. You want to have a big green button with "Proceed to Checkout" or "Continue" or "Enter your shipping address." You want to push people through the cart page to the checkout, moving them further down the funnel.

Here's a great example. See how all the focus is on the checkout button?

Make sure to show payment methods and security logos. Google has an API autofill address feature that plugs into the checkout, so your customers can fill out their information faster. You want to minimize distractions as much as possible and reduce exit points. You want site visitors to continue through the purchase so you get that initial sale.

In the checkout settings, always use the four-step checkout. It converts the highest, because each field pops out, one-by-one, as they're filling out their information.

Always use your own domain for checkout. It looks much more professional. You can do that now with CommerceHQ. You just need to have SSL enabled on your domain.

THE APPS TO SET UP

I't's easy to get caught up installing unnecessary apps, but it's important to keep your store uncluttered and optimized for conversion. Here are the apps you actually need and how they help your store to convert:

161

REVIEW APP

Reviews are critical to have on your Product pages, so you'll want to install a Reviews app. You can have images from your customers with star ratings and, of course, the review text itself. Reviews can increase conversion rates by 1%–2%, so you want to have reviews on every single Product page that you're sending traffic to. Reviews are located at the bottom of your Product page.

You want to have reviews like this all over your store:

WHAT OUR CUSTOMERS SAY...

★ ★ ★ ★ ★
Cat Paw Ring and Earrings

★ ★ ★ ★ ★
Glamorous Black&White Cat Mug

"Thank You Freaky Pet for this very cute cat Jewellery. I love them!"

- Marnie

"I love to drink my morning coffe out of this classy mug and at the same time, support a great cause."

- Anna

Putting reviews on your Product page is a must, but putting them on your Home page helps a lot with conversion rate, also. You can hire someone on Fiverr.com to create a review banner for your Home page.

BUNDLE APP

Bundle offers help increase your average order value (AOV). Instead of buying one item, customers will be offered better deals when they buy more. You can say, "If you buy one, you will save $X, buy 3 and save $Y, or buy 5 and save even more!" Show them how much they're saving, and what percentage discount they're getting with each bundle offer. You can also split test related products being visible or not, on or off. These are extra items related to the product niche at the bottom of the product page.

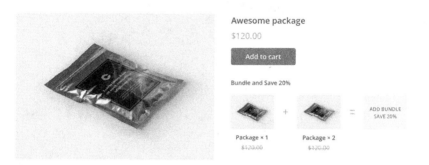

Sometimes it works better to *not* show related products, so the customer is not distracted from checking out. But split test it to see what works best for you. Make the font for the product price very small and light gray, as this little hack can improve conversion rates as well.

UPSELL APP

The built-in upsell app with CommerceHQ allows you to offer discounts and offers to customers after they checkout. On the 'Thank You' confirmation page after ordering, customers are presented with an automated coupon code with a countdown timer. This urgency and deep discount urges customers to take action again, by going back into the store and buying something else. This app alone can drastically increase your store revenue by 10–20%. You can also cross-sell additional products on the Cart page. Showing related products to the niche your customers are interested in will help increase average order value. Test it out with your own store to see big improvements in revenue from this unique upsell app.

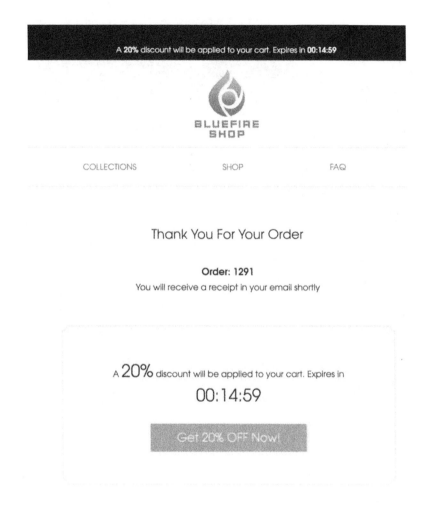

COUPON APP

On the bottom right of the Checkout page, you can put an image of anything you want. Try something like this:

This coupon code banner helps increase your conversion rate because it's giving someone an extra 5% off to complete their order, and adds to the urgency of the offer.

TIMER APP

Having a fifteen-minute countdown timer on the Cart and Checkout pages is powerful. This increases urgency in your potential customers to finish checking out with their order. This is a simple marketing tactic that plays on people's FOMO (fear of missing out).

Your order is reserved for 00:11:25 minutes!

(1) Contact information

Email Address

Continue to Shipping Address

(2) Shipping Address

(3) Shipping Method

(4) Payment

Summary

G Style Men's Sport Watch
Blue $24.99 x 1
1 $24.99

Gift Card Code   Apply

Insured Shipping $0.00

Total $24.99

PRINT-ON-DEMAND APP

Print-on-demand apps are another way to do fulfillment, which is nice, because everything is printed and shipped from the US. With CommerceHQ, we've integrated with CustomCat, a print-on-demand partner located in the US, meaning our orders are printed and shipped directly from the States to our customers, without us having to hold inventory. Orders can arrive to your customer in seven days or less, and there are a wide variety of products to choose from. They have t-shirts, hoodies, leggings, mugs, artwork, phone cases, hats, and more. You have unlimited design options here, and you can set yourself apart from the competition with custom designs.

The CustomCat app itself is very simple to use and navigate:

1. You select the product category, then the product itself.
2. You select the colors and options you want to offer.

3. You choose the price and the 'compare price.'

4. You upload your artwork, and you're all set.

What's great about our print-on-demand app, is that it allows you to upload different artwork for different color shirts. So if I had a black shirt and a white shirt, I would have different color designs so you could see them correctly—for example, white font on a black shirt or black font on a white shirt. Pretty cool feature right?

In addition, we have beautiful mock-ups for print-on-demand. These mock-ups show your product on the t-shirt, so that your Product pages will look great and convert well.

LEAD CAPTURE APP

Exit pop-ups are windows that appear when a user tries to exit your store. By offering a coupon code at exit, you can capture people's email addresses for further follow-up. This app is great for building a list of people interested in your store, but who aren't quite ready yet to buy from you. Email them daily with offers and content so you can covert more traffic into sales.

ZAPIER

Imagine an app that acted like a bridge between two pieces of software. That's exactly what Zapier does. Zapier allows us to connect to thousands of third party apps. We can push multiple types of data and information from one software to another.

The main way we use Zapier is to link to an email marketing platform. For example, you can connect Zapier to CommerceHQ and Aweber. With this "zap," you can send customer email addresses from CommerceHQ to Aweber for marketing purposes. Then you could email offers and discounts to your customer list so that they come back and buy again.

Email marketing is one of the main reasons why you would use Zapier, as it can greatly increase the LTV (lifetime value) of your store. LTV is the average amount a customer will spend over their lifetime interactions with your store. So if a customer comes back to your store multiple times, the LTV increases. When you know how much your customer is worth, you'll know how much you can spend acquiring them. You can use email marketing to increase your customers' LTV, and this will allow you to be more aggressive when scaling your ad campaigns, spending more to acquire new customers, and beating your competition.

zapier Developer   My Apps   Zap Templates   Documentation   Log In   **Sign Up**

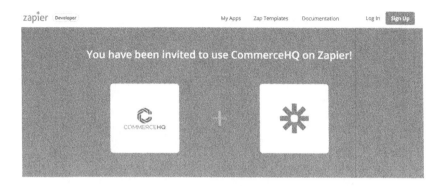

You have been invited to use CommerceHQ on Zapier!

COMMERCEHQ

CommerceHQ is an e-commerce tool that allows you to sell easily.

YOU WERE INVITED BY: INTERNAL@COMMERCEHQ.COM

The CommerceHQ team invites you to test their Zapier integration before it's available for everyone. Neat! Accept the invite and build a Zap with CommerceHQ to get started.

⚡ If you know and trust the developers behind this email address, then this invitation should be safe to accept. This app has not been reviewed or approved by Zapier for functionality or security.

Login to Accept Invite

Sign Up to Accept Invite

THE COPY IN THE EMAIL

When we look at the customer journey after they visit your store, there are several interactions you make before and after they checkout. If someone visits your store and doesn't buy, you can start sending abandoned cart emails to recover the purchase. After someone buys from your store, you send a confirmation email with the invoice. You will be sending weekly or monthly email promotions to your customer list to increase your LTV. These interactions before and after purchase should be set up in advance of running any traffic.

ABANDON CART SEQUENCES

With abandon cart sequences, you'll want to set things up so that you're capturing lost traffic and sales. Inside CommerceHQ, you get access to perfected abandoned cart email templates. Set this up before sending traffic to your store. The goal is to send between three to seven emails to save abandoned carts and convert lost sales. Send the first email ten minutes after the abandoned cart and offer them free shipping. Send the second email five hours after the abandoned cart, offering them 10% off. Send the third email one day after they abandon the cart, offering them 20% off, and saying that it's their last chance. This works incredibly well. You're going to see conversion rates of at least 4% to 5%. In the screenshot below, we saved $40,000 in abandoned cart sales, just by having three emails set up:

It's all done through the CommerceHQ app, like a wizard. You can select from email templates, subject copy, headline copy, body copy, and a call-to-action button. You can also customize the look and feel of the email, what it says, and when it's sent out. You can add as many emails as you want.

THANK YOU EMAIL

In the email confirmation after someone buys from your store, you want to mention that it could take between two to three weeks for their order to arrive because of backorders, especially if you're shipping from China. You need to manage each customer's expectations so they don't freak out and try to get a refund, because they expect two-day shipping like Amazon Prime or something unrealistic like that. The average shipping time should be around two weeks with ePacket from China. But we'll get into that in another chapter.

Another cool hack is having a 'thank you' email with video link. Not a lot of people do this, but it works great to encourage people to buy more from your store. You can hire someone on Fiverr to make an amazing 'thank you' video for your store.

You can have a video like this on the thank-you page after someone buys, with a person saying something like, "Hey! Thanks so much for shopping with us. Your order is being packaged up right now, and we'll get it out to you soon. But in the meantime, here's an additional 20% off coupon, so come back and shop with us right now. We'll give you 15 minutes to use it. Hurry…before the timer runs out!"

That 'thank you' page video hack will help increase the average order value of your store by getting people to make a second purchase. You can even do a professional 1-800 voicemail. So with the phone number you get from Grasshopper.com, you can get someone on Fiverr.com, like this person, who's got an incredible voice, to do a voice-over for a recording saying something like this: "Hello. Thank you for reaching yourstore.com. We are very busy with customers at the moment, but please leave your name and email address and we'll get back to you within twenty-four hours."

THE METHODS OF PAYMENT

Let's make sure you can get paid.

In order to receive payments from your customers and transfer cash to your bank, you need a merchant account, also known as a payment processor. Many processors have strict rules when applying, and there are only a few that allow you to sign up and start taking payments on day one. Stripe and PayPal are two of the best in the world. The sign up is simple and easy. Simply create an account with either or both, fill out all your details, and you can start receiving payments straight away. Let's dive into both processor options with the pros and cons of each.

STRIPE

Stripe is the go-to payment processor right now, because of its seamless integration with most software, tools, and platforms. The speed and ease of sign-up allows you to start selling products on day one and to start receiving transfers to your bank on day two or day seven, depending upon where you're located in the world. Stripe customer support is top notch, and rarely will you run into any issues with your account. Stripe charges roughly 3% per transaction, so make sure to include that in your ROI sheet.

As long as you keep your chargeback rate low, under 1%, Stripe will be more than happy to keep your account open and monies flowing. Chargebacks are when customers call up their bank or credit card company and ask for the transaction to be reversed. To avoid chargebacks, be sure to respond to your customers within twenty-four hours or less, because if they don't hear back from you about their order, they will most likely chargeback.

After working with Stripe for so many years with so many stores, I can tell you they are top in class. I highly recommend you start with them on your store. Although, if you are running heavy international (INTL) traffic, you will want to have PayPal as a payment option as well.

PAYPAL

PayPal is also very easy to set up and start with. You can begin taking payments straight away, and transfer cash to your bank at any time. They also charge roughly 3% in transaction fees, and you will find this is a standard rate with most processors. PayPal is a 'must have' if you are running INTL, because most people in the world have access to it.

The main problem with PayPal is that they are very sensitive to disputes. Meaning, if a customer disputes with PayPal before emailing you, it can be a nightmare. If you have too many disputes over time, PayPal can, and will, freeze the funds in your account. I've heard horror stories of people losing hundreds of thousands to PayPal with funds locked up, seemingly forever. There was even a class action lawsuit, where PayPal lost and had to pay out everyone who had funds frozen in the past five years.

Now, it's not all fire and brimstone with PayPal, because using them as a processor can increase your conversion rate, especially when you start to send international traffic and sales from around the world. If you are going to use PayPal, be sure to transfer funds to your bank account daily and upload tracking numbers from your store orders daily as well. This will protect you from having your funds tied up or limited, and it will keep PayPal happy, because they want to make sure you are a legit business. If you don't upload tracking numbers daily into PayPal, expect an account freeze or limitation. Use PayPal at your own risk.

BEST OF BOTH WORLDS

If you can manage PayPal correctly, then it's worthwhile having both Stripe and PayPal as payment options on your store. Giving people more options to pay can increase conversion rate. So it's worth a test. Just remember the risks, pros, and cons for each payment processor, as mentioned above. If you run into any obstacles, you now know how to handle them. It's smart to have at least one backup payment processor on hand at all times, just in case your main one gets frozen or encounters a rolling reserve or hold back.

Managing cash flow is an important part of the business, and you must stay on top of it. You should be checking your bank accounts at least once per week to make sure you are getting paid. The last thing you want is for your payment processor to stop transfers for a dumb reason like filling out paperwork, etc. Master cash flow and your business will thrive!

THE WEBSITE
CONVERSION CHECKLIST

I know you're super excited to go 'live,' but there are a few things you'll want to check before you start spending your hard-earned cash. When you have your products all lined up and ready to go, the last thing you want is a broken website. Your traffic needs to flow seamlessly through the funnel and end with a sale. If you scale up traffic to a store that is not optimized yet, you risk throwing money down the drain.

PAGE LOAD SPEED

Page-load speed is critical for conversion rate with Ecommerce stores. Luckily, if you use CommerceHQ, you don't have to do much with this, as we're always optimizing on the back end; but it's really important, because one second more load time means you could be losing 10% in conversion rate. So it's essential that pages on your store load as quickly as possible, on all types of devices. Customers are very impatient, and those extra seconds could mean that they don't think the site is working, or that it's taking too long and they get bored. At CommerceHQ, we aim for under two seconds. That's our ultimate goal for maximum conversion rates. You can actually test your product-page speed at websites like GTmetrix.com or WebPageTest.org.

IMAGE COMPRESSION

Image compression is the easiest way to make your pages load faster. If you're going to put a lot of images on your store's pages, make sure they're compressed and small in file size. You can use TinyPNG.com to compress images. Try to get your images below 100 kilobytes each. And only use JPEG images on your store.

HOTJAR

Hotjar (www.hotjar.com) is a powerful piece of software that you can get for just $30 a month. It records user sessions of people visiting your store. You can watch your visitors' every move on your store, so you can see where the leaks are, and why they aren't buying. Maybe there's an issue with the store, or there's some reason they're not able to click or check out easily. Maybe they get lost somewhere. It's a great way to see what people are doing so you can fix any holes in your business and on your store.

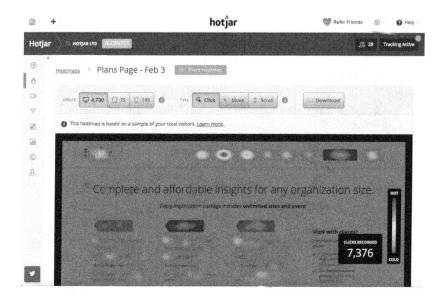

ACTION PROMPTS

1. Research an available domain name using the keywords mentioned earlier, and purchase it for ten dollars right now.

2. Sign up to Fiverr and hire someone to make a professional logo for your store.

3. Set up your store, settings, apps, navigation, and theme using CommerceHQ.

4. Create Stripe and PayPal accounts, then link them to your store so you can start taking payments right away.

5. Test your store fully to make sure your customers can add to cart, checkout and purchase. Create a $1.00 test product, then refund yourself after the test.

THE SELECTION
OF PRODUCTS

THE ECOMMERCE
BUSINESS MODELS

THE OVERSEAS MODEL

Imagine being able to sell products and receive money first, before ever purchasing any inventory or stock. This is the beauty of our business model. Team up with vendors in China, who will send orders directly to your customers. There is no risk of having to buy product inventory up front and getting stuck if it doesn't sell. You only buy products for your customers after you make the sale. It's rare to have a business with such low overhead and risk.

The number one website to source and fulfill products for your customers is AliExpress.com. Not having to buy in bulk, and being able to order one product at a time, limits your risk dramatically. Testing tons of products has never been easier because of AliExpress. com. There is so much selection for any type of niche you can imagine, all right there at your fingertips.

We like to find great vendors on AliExpress, and then start building a relationship with them for deeper discounts and faster shipping. Sometimes they will have Skype so you can chat with them but, in most cases, they will have another chat tool called WeChat. WeChat is very popular in China, and most people use it there to communicate with each other. You can install it for free at https://web.wechat.com.

Now there are downsides to this business model. The most glaring one is the long shipping times from China to the US or other parts of the world. There are different shipping options to choose from, but select the one with the lowest cost and no more than two weeks of delivery time. That is why customer service is very important with this model. You must have staff replying and reassuring your customers that their products are on the way. You can give out tracking numbers when requested, so that they can watch it being dispatched, and check on the estimated delivery time.

THE PRINT-ON-DEMAND MODEL

Back in 2013, I got started with print-on-demand products using

Teespring.com, and I made one million dollars in my first year of business. I learned how to market and sell physical products because of my t-shirt business. It was the first time I used Facebook ads and saw the raw power of the platform. For print-on-demand, the year 2013 was the closest thing to printing money. You could toss up a few t-shirt designs, and most of them would work really well.

They also had time-limited campaigns where you would only be able to purchase for a few days, which created urgency. On the ad side, we would bid $1.00 CPC and have a budget of $1,000. The ROI was huge. Between 100–200%. The 'good ole days.' But don't worry, print-on-demand still works well. You just have to be smarter about it.

Nowadays, you can host your print-on-demand products on your own website. Through apps, you can send designs and orders to print-on-demand fulfillment houses that fill your orders on demand.

With print-on-demand, it's all about the design. You will need to test around ten to thirty designs to find one winner. To find a designer, you can search many different sources. You can find designers from Fiverr, Upwork, or 99designs. You'll have to go through a few to find one you like at a good price point.

You want to focus on scalable designs, those that can be replicated easily into other segments of the market. This means essentially using the same design, but with different niches. This is called horizontal scaling and is highly effective. Here's an example:

This shirt is for people who are born in February, but you could easily make a similar design for every other month in the birth year. Very smart, indeed. You can take a design and scale it across different months or ages, or multiple different things. That's what I like to do when I use print-on-demand. Take a design and see how you can scale it easily, just like this example here with the birth months. Look at how simple this design is—just one color only, which reduces printing cost.

Here are the best t-shirt niches to try:

1. Engineers

2. Gamers
3. 2nd Amendment
4. Bikers
5. Mechanics
6. Grandparents
7. Christianity
8. Veterans
9. Nurses
10. Firefighters
11. Police
12. Photography

Be very careful with political designs though, because Facebook is cracking down on those ads and banning accounts. You don't want to go down that route, even though they do very well due to the controversial nature and all the comments you get on the ads.

Because the world of design is so vast, it's best to see what's working in the marketplace, and what sort of designs work for each niche. Always use products that have done well as inspiration and guidance as to what you should be doing.

Next, I will dive into where to find these hot and proven products, and how to add them to your store.

THE SECRET TO PROVEN PRODUCTS

re you ready to start filling up your store with proven products? I'll show you exactly how to select, source, and load products up on your store fast. This is critical because 80% of your success or failure has to do with the products you select.

It's a good idea to read this chapter a few times to understand the process for selecting proven products. I'll cover pricing, product research methods, product tips, and print-on-demand. When you first start adding products to your store, you want to take the path of least resistance. Finding completely original products, or even creating your own products that sell, is very difficult. You don't want to place giant hurdles in front of yourself, because it can be disheartening and damaging to your business if those products don't work out. So this is why we take the piggyback approach. We see what's working in the marketplace and sell products that we know customers will buy, because they're already buying them from somebody else.

Newer products will always outperform old ones that are saturated in the marketplace. So you should always look for products that have been recently launched or viewed in the past three to seven days. Any more than that and they could be too old or saturated. You're looking for fresh products that most people haven't seen yet. Aim for broad generic products that can reach multiple niches and audiences.

The best niches to focus on include kitchen gadgets, electronics, beauty/fitness, jewelry, and fashion. People have always bought these types of products and always will. It's human nature. Now, when you're selecting products, make sure they fall into one of those proven niches or categories. They should be hard to find as well. You shouldn't be able to easily find the products in any local store or Walmart. They need to be unique, special, and trendy.

Now how do you find proven products? Well, there are a few different methods you can use.

FACEBOOK METHOD

The first method uses your own Facebook News Feed. When you log in to Facebook, the first thing you see is the News Feed. You can type in keywords like "get it now" or "free shipping" and then click on Videos at the top to see all the video ads. You want to find video ads with a ton of engagement, and make sure you Like the pages the ads are hosted on, because then you'll start seeing their ads in your News Feed. This will allow you to track other successful stores and see what products they're launching week to week.

Here's an example of a best-selling product with video ad. You will notice it has 3.6 million views, 8,500 Likes, 1,000 Comments, and 1,200 Shares. Wow!

Collapsible Water Bottle   Like   Comment   Share

Tastemade   Follow   8.5K   1,022 Comments   1.2K Shares

The more views, Likes, Shares and Comments versus when it was launched, the better. Recent comments will tell you if the ad is truly still active and making money for that advertiser. If you see comments posted within the last one or two hours, that means the ad is still running and profitable.

←   **Comments (478)**

New ▾

Excellent

Like · Reply · 4h

ohhh

Like · Reply · 4d

wow

Like · Reply · 1w

increible

Like · Reply · See Translation · 1w

You only want to run products that are still active and being sold right now. If you can find a product launched within the past seven days with over 500,000 video views, that's a big winner that you should test. With image ads, you only want to test products that you've seen with ads over 10,000 Likes.

Be careful selecting products that were launched more than 30 days ago, because they are most likely saturated by competition, and your conversion rate will be low. You want to give yourself the best possible chance of finding a winning product. Most people find a winning product after testing a batch of 20–30 proven products.

It's a very simple process that takes some time, but you can find 20–30 proven products fast. And if your ads are targeted correctly, you will find your first winning product and start to scale it up. Like turning on a light switch, you will know when you find a winner, because the sales will start flying in. Then the next thing you will have to worry about is fulfillment, which I cover in a later chapter.

You can find all these proven products on AliExpress.com. Everything is sourced from China, so you can truly maximize margins and profits. Vendors on AliExpress will ship products directly to your customers for a very low shipping fee. Essentially, you are eliminating the middleman and going directly to the manufacturer.

Look at the example below. In just three weeks' time, this ad got 16,000 Likes, 800 Comments, and 7,000 Shares. Do you think this advertiser was profitable? Absolutely. Why would you scale an ad so much without it being profitable? These are the types of products you want to be loading up on your store and testing with Facebook ads.

Best For Family's Safe Travel

I Want One Too   Follow

Like   Comment   Share

16K   797 Comments   7K Shares

EBAY

The second method is using eBay. Go and explore ebay.com. It's totally free, and you are able to search for keywords and look at the most frequently sold items within the past seven days. You can even search by country as well. Here is a search in the United States using the keywords 'as seen on tv.'

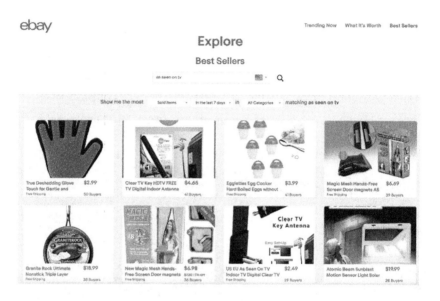

You can easily see the top-selling products that are working right now on eBay. The key is finding products that haven't been seen yet on Facebook, because this means there is no competition yet. So you want to test those ASAP. Be careful that the products you find do not have a patent that you could potentially be infringing on.

ADVANCED SEARCH METHOD

Here's another way to use eBay to find products. It's the advanced search method. (Visit ebay.com/sch/ebayadvsearch.) This tool allows you to see what's hottest right now on eBay, quickly and easily.

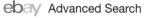

ebay Advanced Search

Home > Buy > **Advanced Search**

Advanced Search

Items	Find Items
Find items	Enter keywords or Item number
On eBay Motors	kitchen gadget
By seller	All words, any order
By item number	Exclude words from your search
Stores	See general search tips or using advanced search options
Items in stores	In this category:
Find Stores	All Categories

Search

Search including
- Title and description
- Completed listings
- Sold listings

Price
- Show items priced from $ ___ to $ ___

Buying formats
- Auction
- Buy It Now
- Classified Ads

Condition
- New
- Used
- Not Specified

1. Start by typing in your keyword at the top, like "kitchen gadget"
2. Search including: Sold listings
3. Buying formats: Buy It Now
4. Condition: New
5. Located in the United States

Click search, and it's going to show you all the top products that are selling right now on eBay.

Kitchen Tools Gadgets Vegetable Fruit Peeler Parer Julienne Cutter Slicer Orange
Brand New
★ ★ ★ ★ ☆ 4 product ratings

$3.75
Buy It Now
+$14.31 shipping
Free Returns
View similar active items
Sell one like this

From United States

Citra Sipper Orange Juice Citrus Spout Sipper Kitchen Tools Gadgets (FREE SHIP)
New (Other)

$5.99
Buy It Now
+$14.21 shipping
View similar active items
Sell one like this

From United States

NEW- Stainless Steel Kitchen Utensil Set - 9 Piece Gadget Tool Cookware Set
Brand New

$19.90
Buy It Now
Calculate Shipping
View similar active items
Sell one like this

From United States

Taco Maker Press Fried Taco Shells Mold Crisp Deep Fryer Kitchen Tools Gadgets
Brand New

$7.12
Buy It Now
+$14.38 shipping
Free Returns
View similar active items
Sell one like this

From United States

If you see a product in these lists that you haven't seen yet on Facebook, it's a great candidate to test, because there's no competition and no saturation yet for that product. So jump on it fast, load it up to your store, and see if it's a winner for you.

AMAZON

Now let's talk about the third method: UnicornSmasher.com. You can download this free plug-in and browser extension tool for Google Chrome browser.

Within twelve seconds, you can see what's selling the most on Amazon. Type in a keyword, click on the plug-in icon at the top right of your browser, and it's going to pop out a window with a bunch of data. It shows you the estimated revenue per product per month. We typically look for products that have over $10,000 revenue per month. These are great products to test with Facebook ads.

Again the key is to find products that haven't yet been seen or launched on Facebook. When you show a proven product to a brand-new audience, the conversion rates are a lot higher, because it's something fresh that people haven't seen before. Cross-platform product research is key if you want to find products that give you massive ROI, 3x or higher. You will want to scale them fast once you find them, before competition steps in. The first to the punch always wins in this business.

Take the time to find proven products and make sure your margins are healthy, so that when you scale, you can be more competitive by either dropping price, offering discounts, or bundling offers. All these tactics will help you increase sales revenue exponentially.

Here's an example product found on Amazon using Unicorn Smasher.

This screenshot is from AliExpress.com, which shows that you can fulfill this product for just $1.74 plus shipping. You could sell this on Facebook for $14.95 plus shipping, an 81% margin. So this is a great way to find products that are working extremely well on Amazon, but maybe have not been seen yet on Facebook. Those are the ones you want to test.

COMMERCE INSPECTOR

The next method uses a Google Chrome plug-in called Commerce Inspector. Using this, you can track the most successful Ecommerce stores with ease. It's a free tool that allows you to see what recent products are being launched by any Shopify store. Very powerful. You can use this tool in conjunction with Facebook ads you find in the News Feed. If you see a store with multiple proven products again and again, that's a very successful store you want to track with Commerce Inspector. You will start picking up on product trends and get a feel for what's working now.

After a few weeks, you will start to know which products are truly new and which products have already been saturated by the competition. You will develop it like a sixth sense, immediately spotting product opportunities as they arise using all these search methods and tools.

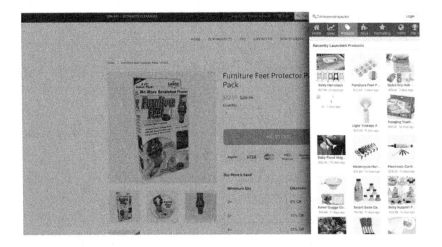

To use Commerce Inspector effectively, visit a popular Shopify store and load up the app by clicking the icon in your browser. Then click on the Products tab. It's going to show you recently launched products. You can track what products big stores are launching on a daily and weekly basis. You want to focus on products launched four, five, or six days ago. Under a week is ideal. This is truly amazing data at your fingertips. You want to follow the stores with big Facebook ads that are doing well, so you can test their new products on your store as well. This method works extremely well.

PEXDA

The last product research method uses a website called Pexda.com. It consolidates proven products for you with lots of details. Pexda shows you product margin, pricing, and profit estimates. It even links you to the vendor on AliExpress. It also shows you who else is selling the product on Amazon and eBay, to give you a good grasp on the competition. Pexda even shows you how to target the product successfully with real audience examples. If you ever get stuck on targeting your Facebook ads, Pexda will give you interests, age range, location...everything. It helps you get started so you can launch ads right away without any guesswork. Not only will it help you with targeting, but it also shows you Facebook video ads for the products. You can download these video ads directly and edit them to make them your own. However, never directly copy someone else's ads or risk getting shut down due to copyright infringement with Facebook.

The best part about this software is that it gives you a product campaign roadmap from end to end. It tells you where to source the product, how much to sell it for, and how you're going to sell it. Pexda is great for people who are struggling or having a hard time getting started with products. It's going to assist you a lot to help in figuring out how to target those products.

They also have an alternate package, that gives you access to more exclusive products that are doing well and have been recently seen on Facebook. You can see products that were launched just a few hours ago. Give it a try—it will be worthwhile, because you're only one winning product away from six figures per month with your online store.

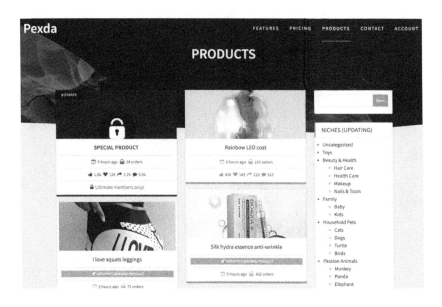

Please be very careful with trademark products. You can find similar products with no logos. Just do a bit of research on AliExpress and make sure you aren't infringing on anything. Never run ads or traffic to products such as Stars Wars or Batman that are trademarked.

THE MARGIN IN THE PRICE

Being able to calculate your margin is important, because this determines how much you can spend on ads and remain profitable. Price is a lever that you move up and down until you hit a sweet spot. For example, if your product is very popular, but the price is too high, you may get a lot of 'add-to-carts,' but no sales. If your price is too low, you may get a lot of sales but find that your margin is too low, so you are not covering your ad and fulfilment costs. Aim for at least 60% margin (profit before ad spend divide by revenue). Make sure you have at least $15 to $20 profit before ad spend, so that scaling will be much easier for you.

FREE PLUS SHIPPING

'Free plus shipping' used to be all the rage. Everyone tried to make money with this method, which is to give the product away for free, but charge $9.95 for shipping. Their cost on the product would be $2–3 leaving a $7–8 margin. But you can't scale with margins this low. You have to sell a ton of volume to make any profits. Customers have also become aware of these offers and know that it's not really 'free,' but that the shipping cost is the price of the product.

So, $10.00 (revenue) - $3.00 (fulfillment) = $7.00 (gross profit) - $5.00 (ad spend) = $2.00 (net profit).

The upside is that it appeals to the impulse buyer. Most customers don't fret over $9.95, so there is less resistance or fear when purchasing. They are also unlikely to refund or go to their bank and chargeback $9.95. But don't expect them coming back to your store and buying retail priced products. The quality and LTV (lifetime value) of these customers are very low.

MOST POPULAR PRICE RANGES

The highest revenue stores on CommerceHQ, that do more than six figures per month price their products between $19.99 and $49.99. The most popular price across the board is $24.99 plus $4.99 shipping. The reason for this is that most purchases made on your store will be impulse buys. Someone seeing your ad on Facebook, clicking the link, and ordering. The $24.99 allows you to hone in on this impulse-purchase behavior, while at the same time giving you a healthy margin for scaling.

HIGH-END PRODUCTS

High-end products are harder to sell, but if you get a product that people see value in buying, even with a higher price point, then it can be very profitable. For example, drones or camera equipment appeal to customers who are used to paying hundreds to thousands of dollars for those kinds of products.

The downside is that you have to be brave enough to spend

more money on ads to get the sale. Refunds and chargebacks are very important to deal with efficiently, because a faulty high priced product is going to motivate the customer to get his or her money back. The upside is that if you have a hot high end product, you can spend more to get the sale. You also don't have to sell as many products as the lower priced products, because your margins are bigger.

PRINT-ON-DEMAND

Most people start selling t-shirts when it comes to print-on-demand sales. The standard t-shirt is the G200 from Gildan. Everyone's used to buying and wearing these shirts daily. The G200 Gildan t-shirt will give you solid margins, because you're going to be selling it for $22.99 and shipping is going to be $4.95—that's a total of $27.94. It's going to cost you $10 for fulfillment, which leaves a margin of $17.94.

Now let's say it costs you $12 in Facebook ad spend to make a sale. You are left with $6 net profit, which is a 50% return on investment. That's right on the money, and where you want to be. Always aim for 50% ROI net.

So, $27.94 (revenue) - $10 (fulfillment) = $17.94 (gross profit) - $12 (ad spend) = $5.94 (net profit).

If you want to offer long-sleeve shirts, use the G240 from Gildan. It's a great shirt, and sells well, while maintaining solid margins. You can make $20 profit before ad spend if you price it at $29.99 plus $4.95 shipping. You will end up with a 60% ROI if you can make sales for $13 or less, using Facebook ads.

So, $34.94 (revenue) - $15 (fulfillment) = $19.94 (gross profit) - $13 (ad spend) = $6.94 (net profit).

Hoodies are very profitable in the winter. You can sell them between $39.99 and $54.99, which will give you around a $24 profit margin. You will end up with 53% ROI, if you can make sales below $16 cost per conversion (also known as cost per acquisition, or CPA) with ad spend. Use the G185 Gildan pullover hoodie to get those numbers.

So, $44.94 (revenue) - $20.94 (fulfillment) = $24 (gross profit) - $16 (ad spend) = $8 (net profit).

Women's tees should be priced at $24.99 plus $4.95 shipping, giving you a $17 margin before ad spend. You end up with a 54% ROI, if you can make sales below $11 ad cost. Use the G500L shirt for that one. Tank tops sell incredibly well in the summer time, and in January with the fitness niche. We use the 882L Anvil shirt, priced at $27.99 plus $4.95 shipping. You should end up with $19 margin before ad spend and almost 60% ROI with conversion that are less than $12.

So, $29.94 (revenue) - $12.94 (fulfillment) = $17 (gross profit) - $11 (ad spend) = $6 (net profit).

It's critical to run all the numbers on a spreadsheet and make sure you have solid margins and profit before running ads or traffic to any given product. Know your numbers, know your business. Never forget this. By knowing your numbers, you will understand how to optimize things in a better way to improve conversion rate, sales, and overall profitability with your business.

ACTION PROMPTS

1. Find 20–30 products that have been found recently, in the past seven days or less, using one of the search methods mentioned earlier.

2. Make sure you have at least 60% margins on all your products, and price them between $19.99 to $49.99 max for an impulse buy.

3. Focus on broad niches like home and garden, kitchen, DIY, etc.

4. If you can find products that have mass appeal with multiple niches, that's a bonus.

THE LAUNCHING OF ADS

THE FACEBOOK AD PLATFORM

F acebook ads is the most powerful advertising platform in the world. Hands down. It allows you to reach millions upon millions of people all over the world with intelligent optimization towards any of your business goals. Want more sales? No problem, Facebook will find buyers for you. Want more engagement? It's just a few clicks away. Want more views on your videos? Consider it done.

Facebook updates their platform consistently every single month, so it's hard to keep screenshots and training updated with so many changes. While going through the next pages, please keep this in mind. What you see here may not exactly match what you see on Facebook, but the concepts, strategies, and system remain the same as they have for years. The UI (user interface) is what changes most commonly. And every quarter or so during the year, Facebook likes to make an algorithm update, so the key is to A.B.T (always be testing).

Reserve at least 10–20% of your ad spend budget for testing new ad, targeting, and scaling strategies, so you can stay on top of what's working now with Facebook ads. You have to be like a mad scientist, split testing many types of creative, targeting, products and more.

Here's a picture of me at the Facebook office in Toronto, Canada, signing the famous Facebook wall.

There are four main departments in Facebook that you might have to deal with when you use Facebook ads:

- Policy
- Risk
- Advertising
- Quality

First, let's start with Facebook's corporate structure. They have teams of developers that work in different departments. The problem is that, when they push new features or policies through, sometimes things break in other areas, and sometimes that area is inside your ad account. The best thing you can do is try to be proactive by keeping your Facebook ad account clean and not giving any department any reason to flag your account.

FACEBOOK POLICY

Facebook ads have rules and, if you break them, there are consequences.

Facebook ad policy is critical to understand, because the last thing you want is for your ad account to get flagged or banned right when you are trying to scale a winning product.

Some rules include:

- No trademark or copyright images or videos.
- Calling out users like 'are you a single mom, looking to lose weight?' because it's deemed discriminatory.
- No big and unrealistic claims like, 'you will make a million dollars.'
- No 'before and after' pictures. For example: weight loss.

There are many more of these rules that you should familiarize yourself with by reading Facebook's ad policy. It can be found here. https://www.facebook.com/policies/ads/

Best practice with your ads manager is to delete old campaigns, ad sets, and ads that you aren't using anymore in your ad account. Essentially, delete all old products that didn't work in your ad account. You can keep them on the store itself, but you want to keep your ad account clean because you never know what can happen in the future. Facebook could make a policy change and flag your ad account.

Another good habit is to always delete disapproved ads immediately from your ad account. If you leave them sitting in your ad account for a long time, it hurts your backend score with Facebook. Facebook will notify you via email if any ad creative gets disapproved, so just delete them right away if this happens to you. If you do end up losing an ad account, don't bother trying to get it back from Facebook, as it could take weeks or months. Don't waste any time here—just fire up a new ad account.

FACEBOOK RISK

Risk is the last department you want to be dealing with. They are incredibly strict when it comes to your business manager, ad accounts, credit cards, and users. If you must deal with the Risk department, there is relatively small chance you will get your accounts back, because it's their job to stop all scammers and fake accounts. And sometimes you can get caught up in these "sweeps" where they mistake you for a bad character looking to "game the system". If you do ever have an encounter with the risk department, be as polite and professional as possible, and you might just get a pass.

FACEBOOK ALGORITHM

The Facebook algorithm is very complicated, but I'll do my best to simplify and explain it to you. The algorithm is a massive auction with tons of advertisers and competitors trying to get traffic and reach. When you launch an ad, you are trying to 'win' the auction. When you win the auction, your ad gets shown to the right person and, hopefully, that results in your desired action. In Ecommerce, that desired action is a sale.

So what affects your chances of winning the auction?

- Your ad account age. Does it have a history of ad spend and positive feedback on your ads and fanpage?
- Your bid. How much are you betting to win the auction?
- Your CTR (click-through-rate) is vital. It's a big indicator to Facebook as to whether your ad is relevant or not.
- Your ad account history. How many disapproved ads have you had? How many ad accounts have been flagged or banned in your BM? All that history matters with your Facebook back-end score. Every Business Manager and ad account has a back-end score that you can't see. It can affect traffic quality and ad costs.
- Your budget. How much are you spending per day? Bigger budgets will make you more favorable in Facebook's eyes, resulting in better ad placement in the News Feed. This means you can get high-quality traffic.

FACEBOOK QUALITY

User feedback plays a massive role in the success of your business, now more than ever. Every fan page has a score that you can check and see. If your fan page scores below two, that's a very bad sign, and you're going to have issues with traffic quality and traffic cost. Make sure that it's above two; if not, you may want to use a different fan page altogether.

Engagement with your ads—meaning people who Like, share, comment, and tag—is crucial. You want to encourage engagement, and you do that primarily with images and video ads.

Last year, Facebook started implementing quality and user surveys, asking customers for their feedback on the experience with online stores. Comment sentiment analysis was also introduced and played a part in the algorithm. Facebook started monitoring positive and negative comments in ad creative. Bounce rate, page views per user, and time on site also started to become factors.

Facebook also outlawed click bait ad copy, and false or misleading claims started getting your ad accounts banned. We started seeing more user feedback surveys with more comment sentiment taking effect as well. Too many ads on a fan page resulted in low or no delivery. What you want to do now is make a post on your fan page to a blog related to your niche. It doesn't matter where you get the blog post link, but make sure to post at least three times per week on the fan page. This will help with your ad delivery and lower costs.

Facebook also started considering the lifetime value of stores, as in how much total revenue each store generated since they started. Facebook is taking all this data they have from online stores and incorporating it into their algorithm. In the user feedback surveys, Facebook would ask customers questions like: How long did it take for the product to arrive? Were you happy with the product and the experience on this store? Facebook also started buying high-volume products themselves to test out at their offices. This was for advertisers who were spending more than half a million dollars per month on ads. They would check to see whether these stores were legit and had good delivery times

This year, Facebook is taking a lot more interest in the quality of Ecommerce stores and how they're affecting the overall user experience on Facebook itself. They want to make sure their users stay on the platform and are happy.

THE BUSINESS MANAGER
AND AD ACCOUNTS

I n this chapter, I'll be covering exactly how to structure your Business Manager and ad accounts for longevity.

The key to success for your Ecommerce business is launching ads daily and consistently, sending traffic and sales to your store. The best way to test new products is to run them with live traffic using Facebook ads. But, first, you need to understand the basics of how to set up your ad accounts. Here's what the business manager navigation looks like inside of Facebook ads. This is where you access Ads Manager, Page Posts, Pixels, Reporting, Conversions, Audiences, and more.

BUSINESS MANAGER

You always want to use your business manager (BM) account and not your personal ad account or Facebook profile to run ads. The chances of having your account flagged or banned is a lot higher if you use a personal account. Plus, you'll have so much more control with Business Manager. You can create a new account at business. facebook.com.

One personal Facebook profile can create up to two Business Manager accounts. I highly recommend you create both right from day one, so in case one goes down for whatever reason, you'll always have a backup.

AD ACCOUNTS

Next, you want to create as many ad accounts as possible in each BM. Typically, you can only create one or two ad accounts at the start. But you can email Facebook support, or sometimes get access to their chat support to ask for more accounts. Fifty ad accounts is a good number to aim for per BM. It's important to not add a credit card or any other payment method to your ad accounts. You can add a credit card to the business manager, but never add a credit card directly to any ad account. You can simply assign the credit card from the BM to the ad account.

THE MAGIC OF THE PIXEL

The Facebook pixel is a very small image that loads on website pages. It tracks website visitor behaviors, so that you can create custom audiences and optimize your ads more effectively. So when someone visits your store and takes an action, the pixel will fire, sending data back to Facebook. The more conversions or pixel fires that occur on your store, the easier it will be for Facebook to optimize for you.

Years ago, everyone was obsessed with "warming up the pixel," which meant you built up data on the pixel so that Facebook could be more intelligent at guessing who to target or show ads to next. Since Facebook updated to the "new pixel," optimization does not solely rely on the pixel itself. The ad account is now number one when it comes to conversion optimization.

Nevertheless, the pixel is essential because it allows you to create multiple custom audiences of people who took actions on your store, such as people who viewed a specific product page, added to cart, or purchased. You can then use these custom audiences to create the most powerful type of Facebook ads ever: Lookalike audiences.

Install Pixel Code

Install your pixel code ——————————————— Add your events

Add the pixel code to your site so that it loads on each webpage. This is typically done by adding it to the global header of your website.

1 **Locate the header code for your website**

Find the **<head> </head> tags** in your webpage code, or locate the **header template** in your CMS or web platform. **Learn where to find this template or code** in different web management systems.

```
<!-- Example -->
!DOCTYPE html>
<html lang="en">
  <head>
    <script>...</script>
    insert_pixel_code_here
  </head>
```

2 **Copy the entire pixel code and paste it in the website header**

Paste the pixel code at the bottom of the header section, just above the **</head>** tag. Facebook pixel code can be added above or below existing tracking tags (such as Google Analytics) in your site header.

```
<!-- Facebook Pixel Code -->
<script>
  !function(f,b,e,v,n,t,s)
  {if(f.fbq)return;n=f.fbq=function(){n.callMethod?
  n.callMethod.apply(n,arguments):n.queue.push(arguments)};
  if(!f._fbq)f._fbq=n;n.push=n;n.loaded=!0;n.version='2.0';
  n.queue=[];t=b.createElement(e);t.async=!0;
  t.src=v;s=b.getElementsByTagName(e)[0];
  s.parentNode.insertBefore(t,s)}(window, document,'script',
  'https://connect.facebook.net/en_US/fbevents.js');
  fbq('init', '252916734882102');
```

YOUR PIXEL ID

Without the magic of the pixel, you wouldn't know which ads were working. The pixel sends data to Facebook, which you can see in the ads manager reports. You will be able to know exactly which ads are profitable, so you can scale them up. And you will know which ads to turn off because they are losing money.

If you don't have the Facebook pixel placed on your store, you might as well be flying blind because, without the pixel, you will have zero visibility into your metrics, and KPIs (key performance indicators). CommerceHQ makes it incredibly easy to set up your pixel.

Add pixel   Facebook Pixel is Set ∧

Your Facebook Pixel is set!

Facebook Pixel ID:
411520009380382

Remove this Facebook Pixel

THE AD ACCOUNT STRUCTURE

Within all ad accounts are Campaigns, Ad sets, and Ads. Campaigns allow you to set an objective such as Conversions or Engagement. Ad sets are where you target your audiences with demographics such as age, gender, location, and interests. Ads are the images or videos you use to attract people to your online store.

Best practice is to set up one niche or audience type per ad account. Better yet, even just one winning product per ad account. The reason for this is because all the data and optimization work best when you're targeting very similar audiences in the same ad account. The ad account itself will be warmed up and optimized toward the type of audience or people who are clicking, adding to cart, and buying. When you open Ads Manager, you will see the toolbar pictured here:

🖥 Account Overview   📷 Campaigns   ⊞ Ad Sets   🖵 Ads

CAMPAIGNS
The purpose of campaigns is to set an objective, and to tell Facebook

what you want to optimize for. There are many types of campaigns, but only three that we utilize: Conversions, Engagement and Video. You will mainly be using Conversion campaigns, because Facebook does such a great job at targeting people who are more likely to convert. For our purposes, this means those who purchase from your store.

Engagement campaigns are used to boost an ad, to get more Likes, Shares, Comments, and Tags. Increasing engagement on your ad posts can greatly improve your CPAs (cost per purchase). Video campaigns tell Facebook you want to optimize to get the most people watching your videos with ten-second minimum watch times. This type of campaign will also help your ad engagement score and improve CPAs.

With Engagement and Video campaigns, you can start with a

budget of $20 per day, to warm up the ad post with likes, shares and comments. You'll often run a Conversion campaign in parallel because nothing beats it when scaling up. Eighty percent of your sales are going to come from conversion campaigns. Facebook knows exactly who the buyers are, so it will show your ads more often to those people. It's scary how much data Facebook has on its users but, in turn, it is massively powerful for advertisers.

AD SETS

Ad sets are where the real power lies with Facebook ads. You can reach anyone in any niche at any time by targeting your ad sets correctly. First, you tell Facebook what you are optimizing for, which will mostly be Purchases. Then you tell Facebook what age, gender and location of people you want to target, followed by interests or keywords for which people have an affinity or likeness.

You can even select whether your ads are run on Facebook, Instagram, Messenger and several other placements. Want to target iPhone users only? No problem. Want to target new mothers who are into yoga? Easy. The 'world is your oyster' when it comes to targeting on Facebook ads, and the possibilities are endless.

Never mix optimization of ad sets in the same campaign. For example, if you have a conversion campaign you don't want to optimize for clicks or engagement for something else.

Always optimize for purchases. Facebook will optimize correctly and send you buyer traffic. Here's another cool hack to use if you want to hide from your competition to make sure they don't see your ads. Exclude Facebook page admins from your ads sets. Other store owners or advertisers won't see your ads because they're owners of fan pages themselves. We exclude them from our targeting.

ADS

Ads are the lifeblood of your campaigns. The images or videos you use attract the right people to visit your store, check out, and buy. The more ads the better when it comes to optimizing campaigns. You never know what type of image, video, or thumbnail will yield the best results. It's important to split test multiple types of creative (ads) to see what work best.

FAN PAGES

Fan pages you create will house your image and video ads. They're simply a placeholder. Don't be worried about gaining Likes or fans. The sole purpose of a fan page is to post ads so you can select them in Ads Manager for launching ad sets and campaigns.

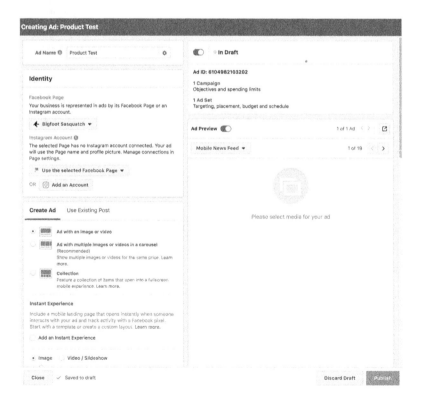

MULTIPLE AD ACCOUNTS

If you have a general store with multiple niches, you can have one ad account per niche. Then share one pixel across all the ad accounts for your store. I'll explain how the plan works. You find thirty products to test, then find one winning product out of that first test batch. Whatever niche that winning product is in will be the only niche you want to focus on with your first ad account. Now you can focus on that one winning product and scale it up.

Do not use that same ad account in the future to test products in different niches. You don't want to muddy up the optimization data. You can launch a new ad account and share the pixel from the first ad account. This way, everything is organized and separated out properly to maximize your conversions and results.

THE AD CREATIVE

The most common ad formats are images that are either 1200x1200 or 1200x628 pixels in size. 1200x1200 image ads, when clicked, expand to a bigger window where the user can see the ad copy, comments, and more. This ad format is highly effective for print-on-demand. 1200x628 image ads are clickable to your store. Meaning if you click on the image itself, it will take users to your store. These types of ads are less commonly used with Ecommerce, as they don't offer as much engagement as 1200x1200 ads, like the image below.

Video ads are by far the most powerful, highest converting, and scalable ad format. The best converting video ads are 1000x1000 pixels in size: a square. This size will take up a considerable amount of real estate in the Facebook newsfeed. Facebook reserves over 50% of ad inventory for video ads only. It's in your best interest to use them with every campaign. Be very careful downloading and using video ads from other advertisers. It's always best to create your own. If you download a video ad, make sure you edit it or send it to someone on Fiverr and have them edit it and add your logo. If you use someone's exact same video ad, you run the risk of losing your Facebook account.

Toes In The Water
July 17, 2017 · 🌐

...

YES!!

After receiving 400 requests on our Facebook page we finally have these available!

Get 50% off and FREE shipping during our launch special.

https://gracecalliedesigns.com/.../infinitus-earring-collecti...

Tag someone who would look amazing in these!

Get yours today!

https://gracecalliedesigns.com/.../infinitus-earring-collecti...

285K   20K Comments 27,151 Shares

HypeDojo

Now you can TREAT signs of aging, relieve ANY chronic pain &
more with this Laser Acupuncture Pen. NO needles! 😎 😎
Get yours here ➡️ www.inspireuplift.com/laserpen

@TAG somebody who should try this ... Show more

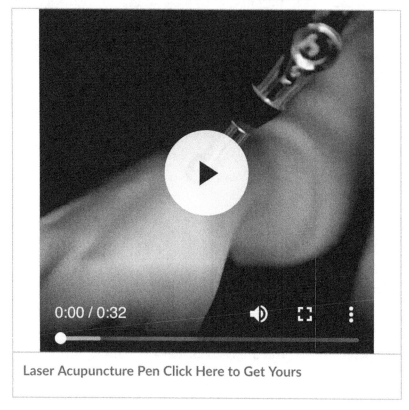

0:00 / 0:32

Laser Acupuncture Pen Click Here to Get Yours

Likes 156591 **Comments** 20645 **Shares** 76385

The best way to create a video ad is to send the product from China
or from your supplier direct to two or three people on Fiverr, and
have them do a testimonial style video. They receive the parcel and
record themselves opening the product and show it off. These types

of video ads convert extremely well, because they show the experience of receiving the product.

The best way to edit your own video ad is to use software like ScreenFlow for Mac or Camtasia for PC. You want to keep the video length below sixty seconds, so you can run on Instagram as well as Facebook. Instagram placement of your ad sets can work extremely well, so test it out. I encourage you to use real customer videos for ads. You could even send your winning product to a few people on Fiverr to create some of these videos for you to use as ads as I mentioned earlier.

Making video ads is time-consuming, so you can use the old faithful 1200x1200 image ads that we've been running since 2015, until you know for sure that you have a winning product. They still work well, and are easy to launch for testing lots of products. This way you don't have to worry about making videos and using editing software. It's always good to split test video ads versus image ads anyway. You never know which is going to work better. And if an image ad converts well with a product, then make the effort to create a video ad as well.

The last type of ad we use is a carousel ad. You can put multiple images or videos in a carousel ad to show off the same product or even multiple products in a collection. I will go into more detail later on regarding targeting, which is what this ad unit is best suited for.

Always put three ads minimum in an ad set so that Facebook can find a winning combination for you more easily. Facebook loves variation, and you will work with their algorithm if you have multiple ads per ad set. You can duplicate the same ad two times for three identical duplicate ads. Each ad will get a different result, and one of the three ads will usually beat the rest in terms of ROAS and CPA. If you are running a video ad, you can set each duplicate ad with a different thumbnail.

THE RULES OF AD SET UP

When you first start launching your ads, you don't want to restrict Facebook too much. Its algorithm is built to find you sales, and it learns as it gains data. If you add too many targeting constraints at the beginning of your ad launch, you will not give Facebook enough space to figure out how to find buyers for you.

Here are some ad set up rules that I use.

AUDIENCE SIZE

Audience sizes vary in different circumstances. It depends on whether you know you have a winning product or not, and how passionate and popular your product's niche is. There are some general guidelines I use in my business.

Your audience size should be between one and five million when testing new products. There are times when you may not have a big enough audience size, and this is okay. Just know that if your product is a winner, your ad might die out faster. You want to find the balance between casting a wide enough net to find your buyers, but not too wide so that you have to spend a lot of money before Facebook finds them. Targeted, but not too targeted. If you want to start scaling a winning product, then you would use bigger audiences of five million plus. By this time, you should know your audience pretty well and be able to target with larger interests. You will be using lookalike audiences at this point.

If you want to do bigger budgets and a lot of daily ad spend, you need to have very big audiences of over twenty million. This is usually when you've hit the goldmine, and you've found yourself a viral product. It's a product that resonates with so many people within your niche, that even if your targeting isn't specific, people still buy.

Audience Definition

Your audience selection is fairly broad.

Specific   Broad

Potential Reach:4,700,000 people ⓘ

AGE AND GENDER

You always want to target ages twenty-two or older because very rarely will you have sales below age twenty-two. Start by targeting women to see if your product is a winner. Women buy more often than men. You can split test ages and genders later after you have a lot of data to work with.

COUNTRY

We send most of our traffic to the US, because they buy the most out of any other country on earth. If you can prove out a winning product campaign in the US, it's time to move to international (INTL) countries like Canada, Australia, New Zealand, the UK, and Ireland. The Nordic countries can be very profitable as well, such as Sweden, Norway, Denmark, Switzerland, Finland, etc. Lastly, test out Worldwide (WW), excluding India and Pakistan, to keep the traffic high quality.

Locations ⓘ   Everyone in this location ▼

United States

 ◉ **United States**

 ◉ Include ▼ | Type to add more locations   Browse

Add Locations in Bulk

PLACEMENT

Your ad placement is where you want your ad to display. There's placement on the actual Facebook site itself, like Facebook News Feed or on the right-hand-side. There's also device placement, such as on desktop or mobile. You always want to start with Facebook Newsfeed only. This will give you the highest quality of traffic to begin testing with. After you get enough data and see what is working best for your product, you can split test different placements, like showing your ads on Instagram, for example. But get all the data in first, so that you can optimize placements properly.

Placement

Automatic Placements (Recommended)

Use automatic placements to maximize your budget and help show your ads to more people. Facebook's delivery system will allocate your ad set's budget across multiple placements based on where they're likely to perform best. Learn more.

● Edit Placements

Removing placements may reduce the number of people you reach and may make it less likely that you'll meet your goals. Learn more.

Device Types

| All Devices (Recommended) ▼ |

Asset Customization ⓘ

1 / 8 placements that support asset customization
Select All

Platforms

▼ Facebook
   Feeds
   Instant Articles
   In-Stream Videos
   Right Column
   Suggested Videos
   Marketplace
   Stories
▶ Instagram
▶ Audience Network
▶ Messenger

●●●●● 🕿   9:41 AM   100% ▬

🔍 Search   ✎

Messages   Active   Groups   Like

Dinner tonight?

Hailey Cook   Mon
Thank you!

Sponsored

Jasper's Market
Check out our best quality locally sourced products

Jasper's Market is now open downtown   Shop Now

More Conversations

Brendan Arnoff

🏠   ▣   ◯   ▨   ⊕

Messenger

View Media Requirement

AUTO BID

Auto bidding means that Facebook will take your daily ad spend set for any given ad set and evenly distribute traffic throughout the day. You will always spend your daily budget, or close to it, when using auto bid. Facebook will automatically bid up and down for you to win more auctions and secure a steady flow of traffic. Eighty percent of our ad sets are auto bid, because Facebook has done such an amazing job at fine tuning their algorithm to balance ad spend with conversion.

Optimization & Delivery

Optimization for Ad Delivery 🛈	Conversions ▼
Conversion window 🛈	1 day click ▼
Bid Strategy 🛈	⦿ **Lowest cost** - Get the most purchases for your budget ☐ Set a bid cap ◯ **Target cost** - Maintain a stable average cost per purchase as you raise budget
When You Get Charged 🛈	Impression
Delivery Type 🛈	**Standard -** Get results throughout your selected schedule More Options

MANUAL BID

Manual bidding is the process of selecting manual bids for your ad sets. You have two options when manual bidding: bid cap and target cost.

Bid cap used to be called max bid. It means Facebook will not bid over the amount you set as the cap to win auctions. Meaning, if your bid is too low, you may not get any traffic delivery at all. If your bid is too high, it might spend too quickly.

Target cost is an interesting bidding method because it sort of combines auto and manual bidding into one. With target cost bidding, you can set an amount that Facebook will try to stay around and average when bidding on auctions for you. This method can work well with lifetime budgets where you set your budget to spend for the ad set over seven, fourteen, or thirty days. Manual bidding is very advanced and not for the faint of heart. You can lose a lot of money very quickly if you don't know what you're doing.

Optimization & Delivery

Optimization for Ad Delivery ⓘ	Conversions ▾
Conversion window ⓘ	1 day click ▾
Bid Strategy ⓘ	◉ **Lowest cost** - Get the most purchases for your budget
	✓ Set a bid cap
	$26.00 per purchase
	We won't bid more than this amount for any individual purchase. You may have trouble spending your budget if this amount is too low.
	○ **Target cost** - Maintain a stable average cost per purchase as you raise budget
When You Get Charged ⓘ	Impression
Delivery Type ⓘ	Standard - Get results throughout your selected schedule
	More Options

CONVERSION WINDOW

The conversion window is the amount of time Facebook will take into account when looking at optimization. You can select between one day or seven days and click or view. If you choose one-day click, for example, Facebook will optimize only with data from the past twenty-four hours of people who clicked on your ad. This data will tell Facebook who to target and show your ads to next. If you can produce more than fifty conversions per week per ad set, one-day click will work well. Less than that and you may want to test a seven-day click. Which means Facebook will optimize with the past seven days' worth of data. It's always good to split test one- day click versus a seven-day click for your winning product campaigns. When it comes to Facebook ads, test like crazy to see what does and doesn't work for you.

SCHEDULE

When it comes to scheduling your ad sets and ads, there are a few hacks to test out with your campaigns. Start new ad sets at three a.m. ad account time zone the next day to get a running start. Most people start new ad sets whenever they feel like it, but doing this can blow out your budget fast. Facebook needs a full day to optimize correctly when using auto bid, so it's important to start ad sets off early in the morning. The reason why we start them at three a.m. instead of twelve a.m. is because not a lot people are awake that early in the morning. So by starting at three a.m. you will have more people clicking and engaging with your ads, meaning lower ad costs and higher conversions. It's really the best of both worlds. A hard rule of thumb is to never launch ad sets after twelve noon ad account time zone.

Start Date 📅 Oct 16, 2018   🕐 3:00AM

Pacific Time

End Date   ⦿ Don't schedule end date, run as ongoing

⦾ End run on:

Ad Scheduling ⓘ   ⦿ Run ads all the time

⦾ Run ads on a schedule

THE DIFFERENT TYPES OF TARGETING

Targeting is not as difficult as you might think. Facebook's algorithm is so powerful that, if you target niche interests big enough for optimization, Facebook will find buyers for you almost on autopilot. You just have to point Facebook in the right direction, and tell Facebook what type of people you are aiming for. Once you start getting sales and conversions, optimization will kick in, and Facebook will find more buyers in your audiences. Don't get caught up wondering if your targeting is on point. It's better to test a lot and test often.

BEST INTERESTS

The best interests can be found using Google search. Focus on finding interests such as magazines, websites, brands, stores, and associations for your product niche. The people who have liked these interests are very targeted and tend to be the most passionate. If you're going to like a magazine about fishing, you probably fish and buy fishing products. You will find great results testing ad sets with these types of interests. Try grouping magazines together, all stacked inside one ad set. Then try the same thing for websites. And on and on. Keep split testing until something hits.

Detailed Targeting

INCLUDE people who match at least ONE of the following ⓘ

Interests > Additional Interests

Field & Stream

Outdoor Life

salt water sportsman

Sport Fishing Magazine

Add demographics, interests or behaviors   **Suggestions** | **Browse**

Exclude People or Narrow Audience

Expand interests when it may improve performance at a lower cost per result. ⓘ

BROAD

Broad audiences are large audiences that are less targeted, hence the name. When you use broad targeting, you're going for quantity, not quality. This type of targeting is best used when you have a broad product with mass appeal that can sell towards a vast number of different audiences. For example, a kitchen gadget could be purchased by all types of people all over the world. The best way to split test big, broad interests, is to try one interest per ad set all by itself. By testing ten to twenty broad interests, you may not be profitable yet, but you will see where the sales are coming from with the specific interests being tested. You can then group together all the best broad interests into one ad set for better results, because Facebook favors multiple interests in an ad set. Broad interests are large in audience size, the average being two million plus.

Detailed Targeting   INCLUDE people who match at least ONE of the following ⓘ

ⓘ

Interests > Additional Interests

Kitchenware

Add demographics, interests or behaviors | **Suggestions** | **Browse**

Exclude People or Narrow Audience

☐ Expand interests when it may improve performance at a lower cost per result. ⓘ

PRECISE

Smaller interests like magazines are considered to be precise targeting. Audience sizes for these interests range between 100K and 500K each. The best way to explore deeper into precise interests is to use the Facebook suggestion tool on the ad set level. Facebook knows which interests are closely related, and what people like the most between them. Using suggested interests will help you uncover new ways of targeting you didn't even think of yet. It will allow you to scale further into more audiences that will expand the lifecycle of your winning product campaigns. You can stack precise interests together in an ad set to get the total audience up into the one million to five million range as suggested.

Detailed Targeting | INCLUDE people who match at least ONE of the following ⓘ

Interests > Additional Interests

Cooking Light

Gourmet (magazine)

| Add demographics, interests or behaviors | Suggestions | Browse |

Taste of Home — Interests

Bon Appétit — Interests

Food & Wine — Interests

Epicurious — Interests

Connection — Saveur — Interests

Allrecipes.com — Interests

Cooking Channel — Interests

Jamie Oliver — Interests

INTERSECT

Intersecting is very useful for finding the most passionate people within a niche. These are people who like two or more interests within a niche. For example, a person who likes 'knitting,' and 'crochet,' and 'sewing machine,' is perfect targeting for selling knitting products. Essentially, you are intersecting multiple interests together to laser target people in the niche. Facebook calls this method 'narrowing your audience.' The key to strong intersect targeting, is to make sure that your audience is still a decent size. Above one million audience size is what you want to shoot for.

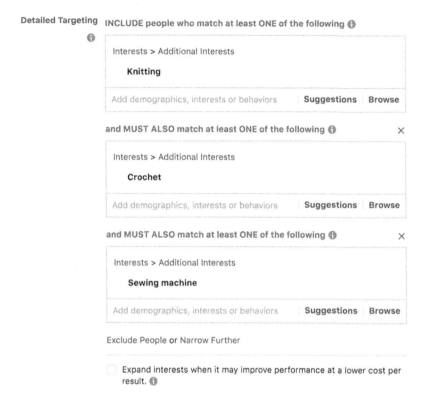

MORE TARGETING EXAMPLES

Let's go over some targeting examples. For a home niche product, you could target a store like HomeGoods and intersect it with housekeeping.

Detailed Targeting INCLUDE people who match at least ONE of the following ⓘ

Interests > Additional Interests

HomeGoods

Add demographics, interests or behaviors | **Suggestions** | **Browse**

and MUST ALSO match at least ONE of the following ⓘ ✕

Interests > Additional Interests

Housekeeping

Add demographics, interests or behaviors | **Suggestions** | **Browse**

Exclude People or Narrow Further

☐ Expand interests when it may improve performance at a lower cost per result. ⓘ

Another great example of intersecting interests would be anyone who likes Bed Bath & Beyond or Wayfair intersected with home furnishings.

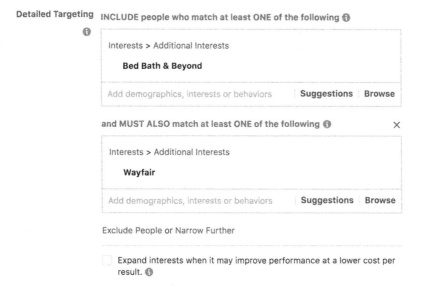

Another example of targeting for a tech gadget-type product would be TechCrunch or TechRadar interests intersected with people who own iPhones.

Detailed Targeting   INCLUDE people who match at least ONE of the following ⓘ

Interests > Additional Interests

TechCrunch

TechRadar

Add demographics, interests or behaviors   **Suggestions**   **Browse**

and MUST ALSO match at least ONE of the following ⓘ   ✕

Behaviors > Mobile Device User > All Mobile Devices by Brand >
Apple

Owns: iPhone 6

Owns: iPhone 6 Plus

Owns: iPhone 6S

Owns: iPhone 6S Plus

Add demographics, interests or behaviors   **Suggestions**   **Browse**

Exclude People or Narrow Further

Expand interests when it may improve performance at a lower cost per
result. ⓘ

When testing new products, you want to be as laser-targeted as possible to give yourself the best chance of making sales right out of the gate. If you get traction with any product, you should immediately move to bigger audiences and start scaling up. Don't get hung up on targeting. Just get out there and launch ad sets every single day. Once you've created your ad and set the targeting, you are ready to go 'live.' It's time to see if you've targeted the right people, and if those people like your product.

THE ROI AND ROAS

You've created your ad and you've gone live! Now what? Once your ads turn on, you'll need to wait and collect data. This is the scary part, because you're spending money on ads and you don't know what is going to work and what isn't.

The first thing you're going to do is set up reporting. Facebook ads manager shows you exactly who clicked, added to cart, and purchased from your ads. You can identify winning ad sets and ads with ease by looking at KPIs (key performance indicators) or metrics, such as CPM, CTR, CPC, budget, spend, ATC, purchase, CPA, ROAS, and more.

Using your reporting, you'll want to analyze your data and gain transparency into your business. Every day, you'll be calculating your two most important metrics, ROI and ROAS. These numbers will tell you how your business is doing. If you're struggling or winning. The image below is what you will see when you click on customized columns in Ads Manager. It will allow you to display custom metrics as mentioned above.

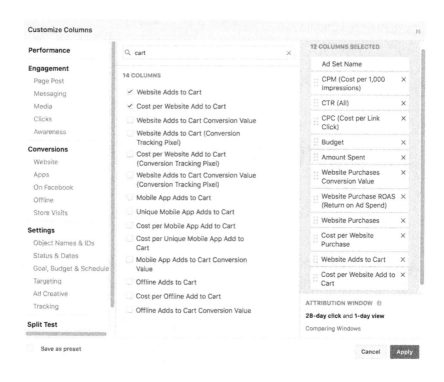

Your ads manager will look like this after you apply the customized reporting.

ROI

You'll want to create a reporting spreadsheet to update every single day. This is your ROI spreadsheet. This ROI spreadsheet is going to tell you how to interpret the data and results. It is your guide to profitability, so you can track and know your numbers inside and out. The goal is that, by glancing quickly at your ROI sheet, you will be able to see where holes are in the funnel. Then you can fix those issues and get back to profitability.

When you take the metrics from Facebook ads manager and input them into your ROI spreadsheet, it should look something like this:

Date	Fulfillment	Spend	Revenue	Profit	ROI	DAY	MARGIN
August.1	7011.76	8,816.67	21,312.64	$5,484.21	62%	Monday	25.73%
August.2	7989.89	4479.44	24,143.71	$11,674.38	261%	Tuesday	48.35%
August.3	11280.69	7963.68	35,216.78	$15,972.41	201%	Wednesday	45.35%
August.4	18354.44	11,717.42	56,476.03	$26,404.17	225%	Thursday	46.75%
August.5	18044.39	11303.8	57,362.00	$28,013.81	248%	Friday	48.84%
August.6	15447.98	13,927.69	55,342.00	$25,966.33	186%	Saturday	46.92%
August.7	16816.35	12,125.66	47,729.48	$18,787.47	155%	Sunday	39.36%
August.8	12339.86	8400.14	33,000.90	$12,260.90	146%	Monday	37.15%
August.9	8323.33	7418.12	24,165.92	$8,424.47	114%	Tuesday	34.86%
August.10	5957.95	6769.7	16,991.18	$4,263.53	63%	Wednesday	25.09%
August.11	3991.19	4,844.97	18,994.42	$10,158.26	210%	Thursday	53.48%
August.12	3738.6	2,931.43	11,539.50	$4,869.47	166%	Friday	42.20%
August.13	8738.99	5,239.32	24,061.02	$10,082.71	192%	Saturday	41.90%
August.14	6112.98	5,430.59	17,802.32	$6,258.75	115%	Sunday	35.16%
August.15	5061.26	4,703.05	15,907.56	$6,143.25	131%	Monday	38.62%
August.16	6797.94	5,091.15	19,346.64	$7,457.55	146%	Tuesday	38.55%
August.17	6786.21	8,424.56	19,732.34	$4,521.57	54%	Wednesday	22.91%
August.18	5905.51	6,342.30	16,724.03	$4,476.22	71%	Thursday	26.77%
August.19	5383.53	3,126.75	15,700.77	$7,190.49	230%	Friday	45.80%
August.20	6585.46	5,172.08	19,626.82	$7,869.28	152%	Saturday	40.09%
August.21	5826.47	5,626.13	19,698.40	$8,245.80	147%	Sunday	41.86%
August.22	5388.88	3,821.63	15,873.91	$6,663.40	174%	Monday	41.98%
August.23	5102.77	3468.66	15,124.37	$6,552.94	189%	Tuesday	43.33%
August.24	5909.93	4414.81	16,914.31	$6,589.57	149%	Wednesday	43.57%
August.25	5711.85	4437.98	15,024.94	$4,875.11	110%	Thursday	32.45%
August.26	2077.33	3918.57	13,904.69	$7,908.79	202%	Friday	56.88%
August.27	5326.73	3126.66	14,365.72	$5,912.33	189%	Saturday	41.16%
August.28	5779.23	3877.06	15,665.63	$6,009.34	155%	Sunday	38.36%
August.29	6471.01	6133.31	16,851.19	$4,246.87	69%	Monday	25.20%
August.30	6005.06	4676.59	15,991.08	$5,309.43	114%	Tuesday	33.20%
August.31	7065.94	5455.45	19,332.98	$6,811.59	125%	Wednesday	35.23%

Here are some simple formulas to help set up your ROI spreadsheet:

1. Profit = Revenue – Fulfillment – Ad Spend
2. ROI = Profit / Ad Spend

3. Margin = Profit / Revenue

Your ROI goals vary at different stages in your business. Businesses that are scaling are often happy with lower ROIs, because their profits increase overall as they scale. As a rule, if your ROI is 50% and above, you're golden.

When I first consult with my clients, I ask to see their ROI spreadsheet. You'd be surprised how many of my students don't even have an ROI sheet! It's a big red flag, and tells me that the business is being run on the fly, blindly. If you don't know how much you made yesterday or last week or last month, how do you possibly think you'll be able to reach your goals and targets? It's a big mistake not to track your numbers, daily. Once you get into the flow of updating your ROI sheet, it will become second nature to you.

ROAS

If there's any metric more important than ROI, it's ROAS (return on ad spend). ROAS is your guiding star, your true north. Without getting a profitable ROAS, you have no hope at scaling your business. ROAS, or return on ad spend, is calculated by dividing your revenue by your ad spend.

ROAS = Revenue / Ad Spend

So if you spent $100 on ads yesterday and returned $200 in revenue, your ROAS would be 2X. If you want to maintain profitability, you have to manage your overall ROAS day in and day out. ROAS trumps all other metrics.

Your reports in FB manager will show ROAS like this:

Amount Spent	Website Purchases Conversion	Website Purchase ROAS (Return

Website Purchase ROAS (Return on Ad Spend) See More

The total return on ad spend (ROAS) from website purchases. This is based on the value of all conversions recorded by the Facebook pixel on your website and attributed to your ads.

$0.00

Now, each quarter of the year will yield different ROAS results. For example, Q1 and Q2 you are likely to get 1.8–2X ROAS overall. But in Q3 and, especially, Q4, sales ramp up. Many millionaires are minted in the last quarter of the year simply because it's gift-buying season and revenues skyrocket. Nothing beats Facebook ads, it's an absolute monster platform that can change your life in a heartbeat. You can scale fast, and it works incredibly well once you have things locked in.

Your main key performance indicator again is ROAS.

I can't say enough how critical this one metric is to your business success: how much you are spending and how much you are making back in revenue daily. That's more important than your cost per conversion, cost per link click, cost per add to cart, or any other metric. ROAS trumps everything.

Once you find a winning product, you should of course optimize for ROAS. For example, if you're going to have revenue of $30 per sale and it costs $7 to fulfill that product, your gross profit is $23 and your margin is 50%. Let's say it costs you $15 to get a conversion using Facebook ads. Now you've got a net profit of $8. That means, to get 50% return on investment you have to do at least 2x ROAS minimum.

$23 - $15 = $8

$8 / $15 = 53%

THE WINNING PRODUCT

L et's talk about winning products now and how to identify them. Your main task is to find just one winning product and scale it up.

A winning product must make sales consistently and be profitable at scale. This means that if you launch 10 ads, at least 3 of them should work. You want to have, at bare minimum, a 30% stick rate. The key is to also achieve a minimum ROAS (return on ad spend) of 2x. So that means you want to be doubling your ad spend with generated revenue.

Most products, if they are priced correctly and have decent margins, will be profitable and scalable at 2x ROAS. Let this be your main key performance indicator (KPI) for your business health.

A winning product is typically something that has been launched or seen within the past three to seven days. New products recently seen in the marketplace in the last week or earlier will always perform the best, because they aren't saturated yet by the competition. Now, you're looking for products that have a lot of video views if it's a video ad on Facebook and over one million views is a great indicator. That means they are likely very profitable and getting scaled quickly, with a lot of ad spend. To reiterate, a winning product should be able to easily hit 2x ROAS or higher at scale.

GOLD PRODUCT

Gold products are found within the past seven days and command high ROAS, over 2.5X. When you find these products, scale them fast before the competition does. It's like hitting the jackpot. They only come around once in a while, but when you find one you will know it right away. Because it's so easy to scale, more than 50% of the ads you launch should stick. This makes scaling up a breeze. ROI on these products can be as high as 100% or more. You can quickly scale up to twenty, thirty, forty, or even fifty ad sets per day and, as long as your ROI holds, you can keep increasing your ad spend.

GOLD PRODUCT

Link Clicks	CTR (All)	Frequ...	CPM (Cost p-...	CPC (Cost per Li...	Budget	Amount Spent	Website Purchases - Conversi...	Website Purchase RO...	Website Purchases	Cost per Website Purchas	Website Adds to Cart	Cost per Website Add ...
492	4.18%	1.10	$11.29	$0.93	$50.00 Daily	$456.54	$12,595.70	27.59	89	$5.13	468	$0.96
1,369	2.55%	1.32	$5.76	$0.71	$50.00 Daily	$967.15	$11,578.11	11.97	79	$12.24	647	$1.49
1,504	2.50%	1.19	$6.30	$0.74	$25.00 Daily	$1,115.46	$9,284.33	8.32	71	$15.71	609	$1.83
774	2.27%	1.31	$5.31	$0.78	$50.00 Daily	$604.85	$7,508.99	12.41	52	$11.63	353	$1.71
546	2.19%	1.07	$12.04	$1.51	$15.00 Daily	$821.94	$7,227.07	8.79	45	$18.27	586	$1.40
1,384	2.26%	2.51	$11.55	$0.80	$25.00 Daily	$1,102.86	$7,095.71	6.43	51	$21.63	172	$6.41
851	3.12%	1.45	$6.21	$0.79	$50.00 Daily	$676.37	$6,982.64	10.32	52	$13.01	780	$0.87
143	1.87%	3.35	$18.32	$3.39	$5.00 Daily	$464.26	$8,982.66	14.36	71	$6.82	78	$6.21
1,219	2.56%	1.10	$6.85	$0.84	$75.00 Daily	$1,026.25	$6,734.90	6.56	44	$23.32	535	$1.92
785	2.47%	1.05	$14.28	$1.59	$8.00 Daily	$1,244.92	$6,559.76	5.27	50	$24.90	290	$4.29
775	3.32%	1.40	$8.51	$1.06	$50.00	$823.03	$6,082.99	7.39	44	$18.71	763	$1.08
147,693 Total	2.31% Per Imp.	2.30 Per Per...	$4.93 Per 1,000...	$1.03 Per Action		$162,417.70 Total Spent	$910,983.82 Total	5.98 Average	6,893 Total	$22.11 Per Action	75,531 Total	$2.02 Per Action

SILVER PRODUCT

Silver products are found within the past thirty days or earlier and hit 2X ROAS, minimum. It could be an old gold product from a year ago that has been recently revived. This could happen because the main niche or audience has been refreshed with new people. These types of products are really your bread and butter. You can run silver products in parallel and stack them, month after month. It's much easier and more common to find these types of products, because there are so many of them in the marketplace.

BRONZE PRODUCT

Bronze products are more than thirty days old and have a low ROAS, around 1.5X on average. Bronze products are not scalable because the numbers will never make sense. You can never get profitable no matter what you do. The product margin might be too low, below 50%, or the CPA (cost per purchase) is always too high. Be careful not to fall into the trap of generating sales with a bronze product by losing money and wasting time. It's a common pitfall people encounter in this business. Profit is king. Don't forget that. If you are trying to scale a product for more than two to three weeks and it's not profitable, time to move on to the next one.

TESTING

You must test between ten and thirty products to find one gold or silver product. It's amazing how much you can earn with just one winning product. Our top members on CommerceHQ do more than six figures per month, and are mostly scaling with just one winning product. If you make $100K in revenue, you can expect $20K–$30K net profit, which is life-changing income. What would you do with all that cash? Below is a similar representation of what someone made in their first two weeks of scaling!

TRENDS TDY YTA 1W 1M 3M CUSTOM

Revenue	Orders	Visitors
$119,812.71	2,891	100,235

THE OPTIMIZING RULEBOOK

Optimizing your ads correctly is the difference between losing money and making money with your store. You want to optimize, or turn off bad ad sets and ads, at least twice per day, once in the morning and once in the later afternoon or evening. We are looking for ad sets that achieve 2X ROAS or higher. Having product margins above 60% will translate to a net ROI of around 50% at 2X ROAS, the money zone. If you can maintain 2X ROAS overall for your ad account, magic happens. You can stay profitable just by managing this one metric.

Here are three rules that will save you money, pain, and time. Make sure you're following these three simple rules daily to get and stay profitable:

1. If no link clicks after $5.00 spent = pause
2. If CPC (cost per link click) is over $2.50 and $5.00 spent = pause
3. If ATC (cost per add to cart) is over $10.00 and $15 spent = pause
4. If no sales after $20.00 spent = pause

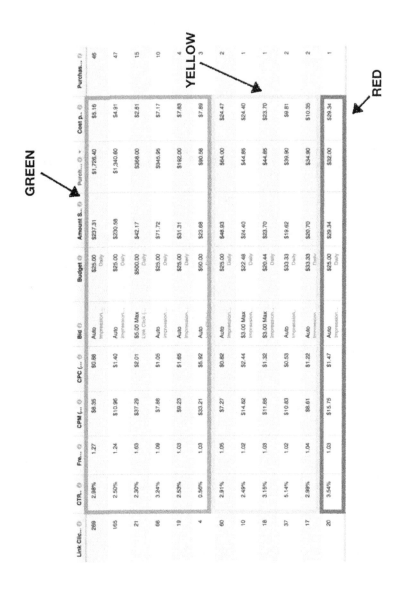

The green box shows ad sets with great ROAS that should be scaled. The yellow box shows ad sets that have borderline ROAS that should be monitored over the next few days. The red box shows an ad set that should be paused because it's not profitable.

Over time, you will develop a sixth sense when it comes to optimization. You will be able to quickly glance at your ad manager and know exactly what to pause and what to scale. Optimization is the key to getting and staying profitable with your business. You must stay on top of the overall ROAS of your campaigns and scale up slowly while maintaining positive ROI. As a rule of thumb, don't launch more than 50% of active ad spend. For example, if I spent $100 yesterday, I wouldn't want to spend more than $150 today. This will help lock in profits while you turn up the volume.

THE CUSTOM AUDIENCE

et's get into the most profitable type of targeting you can do with Facebook ads: custom audiences. You want to start using custom audiences, especially when scaling. A custom audience is a group of people that Facebook creates for you, based on the demographic data you provide. The reason why you want to build up these custom audiences, is because Facebook can use this data to find more people who have a higher probability of buying from your store. The audiences are built from actions that past customers have taken. There are certain steps in the store buying process that are tracked and, as you get more customers who take these actions, they are added to your custom audience. In essence, you are 'building' a list of people who have shown interest in your products.

Audience

NEW AUDIENCE ▾

Custom Audiences ⓘ | Add Custom Audiences or Lookalike Audiences |

Exclude | Create New ▾

So as soon as you find a winning product, you will want to create these key custom audiences:

- Page View: anyone who has viewed any page on your website.
- View Content: anyone who clicked and viewed your Product page.
- Add to Cart: anyone who added a product from your store to their cart.
- Initiate Checkout: anyone who started to fill out the order form.
- Purchase: anyone who purchased a product from your store.
- 95% video viewed: anyone who viewed at least 95% of your video ad.
- Engaged with fan page or ads: anyone who clicked, shared, liked your fan page, or ad.

You can create custom audiences in the Audiences section of Business Manager.

Create a Custom Audience   ×

How do you want to create this audience?

Reach people who have a relationship with your business, whether they are existing customers or people who have interacted with your business on Facebook or other platforms.

Customer File
Use a customer file to match your customers with people on Facebook and create an audience from the matches. The data will be hashed prior to upload.

Website Traffic
Create a list of people who visited your website or took specific actions using Facebook Pixel.

App Activity
Create a list of people who launched your app or game, or took specific actions.

Offline Activity [NEW]
Create a list of people who interacted with your business in-store, by phone, or through other offline channels.

Engagement [UPDATED]
Create a list of people who engaged with your content on Facebook or Instagram.

This process is secure and the details about your customers will be kept private.

Cancel

Facebook will automatically add people to your custom audience after you have created them, so you don't have to worry about updating them. There are many uses for these custom audiences. You can use these custom audiences not only to retarget people with ads, but also to make lookalike audiences, which are the most powerful type of ads on Facebook.

LOOKALIKE AUDIENCES

You can create lookalike audiences from custom audiences after they have a thousand people or more each. For example, if there were 1,000 people who viewed your Product page but didn't buy, Facebook would take that data and create a lookalike audience (LLA). You can create LLAs in the Audiences section of Business Manager.

Actions ▼

Create Lookalike

View Pixel   ⓘ

Edit

Delete

Share

Show Audience Overlap

Lookalike audiences are audiences that are built up of similar people to your custom audience. So for those people who viewed your Product page and didn't buy, Facebook would go out and find people who are likely to also view your Product page, but hopefully, in this case, buy.

Lookalike audiences are large with millions of people in them. They can be extremely profitable. It's like having your own traffic source, made up of people who are very likely to buy your products, grouped in a way that only you can run ads to.

Now, you always want to have interest-based ad sets running in parallel to lookalike ad sets, because they will feed data into the custom audience, which automatically updates the lookalike audiences. The interest-based ad sets are almost like maintenance ads for your custom audience. They keep your custom audience data fresh and relevant.

You can create different types of lookalikes with different percentages. The percentages in a lookalike target different people. They range from 1% to 10%. A 1% LLA would be very targeted and most similar to your custom audience. This is because, the lower the percentage, the higher the likeness to the custom audience. A 10% LLA would be a very diluted version of the custom audience, because the higher the percentage, the bigger the audience, and the less targeted it is. Sometimes, these higher percentage lookalikes work, so be sure to test them.

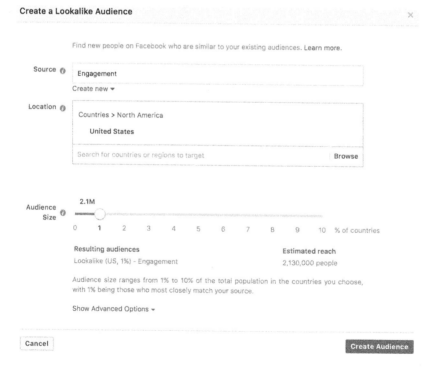

You can do 1%, 2%, 3%, or even advanced ranges like 1–2%, 2–3%, 3–4%. Also, try bigger ones like 1-3%, 3–5%, 5–7%, or 7–10%. It's best to create and split test all of them, because you never know what's going to work with your ads.

Another thing you can do is intersect lookalike audiences with your best broad interests, so people in this ad set targeting will be in the LLA and must 'Like' the interests as well. It's a laser-targeted audience that can work great, if wide-open LLAs are not working well for you.

THE RETARGETING GOLDMINE

R etargeting is when you target people who have seen your ad and indicated interest by taking certain actions. They might have clicked on the ad, or gone to the Product page, or gone to the checkout. As you run ads, you will collect data on who has responded to your ad, and they will start being added to your custom audiences. You will want to start retargeting these audiences after you have at least one hundred people inside each one. When you start scaling, you want to pick up all the lost sales of people who didn't purchase on the first ad, constantly moving them down the funnel to the sale. You can hit them again and again until they buy with different ads, at different times. This is the power of custom audiences. Retarget people at every step of the funnel until they come back and buy.

For example:

- People who visited your Product page within the last three days but didn't add to cart.
- People who added to cart in the last seven days, but didn't buy.

- People who started to fill out the order form in the past fourteen days but didn't buy.
- People who purchased in the past thirty days.

You can set up different types of custom audiences and retarget them all with different ad copy, offers, and promotions. You could offer them a 10% off coupon code or even free shipping. Hit them with different offers and angles at different steps in the funnel, to get them to come back and buy.

For ad creative when retargeting, this is when we use carousel ads. They are the most effective. I'm going to give you a few retargeting methods to test with your campaigns.

THE SMASHER METHOD

The first retargeting method is called The Smasher. We scale our existing retargeting ads by increasing budgets.

You start with $10 budgets and double the budget daily on ad sets with 3x ROAS or higher. Which is average for retargeting because they are so profitable. You can also duplicate the best ad sets three times per day. Many people don't do this, because they're worried about ad overlap in the auction. But we find that it works incredibly well. Test both strategies to see what works best with your campaigns.

TESTIMONIAL METHOD

This method requires a video ad variation. Maybe the first video ad piqued their interest, but didn't get the sale. So try a different ad angle.

Some of the best converting ads are testimonial videos. Stacking video testimonials in the same carousel ad works great as well. It's a simple strategy that establishes trust, authority, and credibility with your prospects. And it focuses on why they need your product. The goal here is to move them from just viewing the Product page to adding to cart and eventually purchasing.

If they saw your initial ad in the past three days, hit them with a long-copy ad post with a 10% off coupon code. Then, for the past seven days' audience, hit them with a video ad and give a free shipping coupon code. Then, if they still haven't purchased within fourteen days, hit them with a carousel ad giving them 20% off.

CUSTOMER LIST METHOD

The biggest retargeting strategy people don't use is to run ads to their customers list. Start running retargeting ads to your buyers thirty days after they made a purchase. Give them time to receive their first order, then hit them again with more products so they come back and buy. This is the most profitable ad strategy in your arsenal. Use it monthly for massive results.

The idea is that 30% of your store revenue should be from repeat buyers. You will see very high ROAS with this method, typically in the range of 5X–10X. Make sure you give your buyers a sweet deal. BOGO (buy one/get one) offers are a great fit for this. You can do a big, time-limited, flash sale once per month, and put a timer on your whole store.

CROSS-SELL METHOD

You could also run email campaigns at the same time to maximize your reach, hitting them not only with ads but with emails as well. Also, you could open a second niche store using CommerceHQ and invite buyers from your first store, cross-selling buyers between stores.

THE SCALING METHODS

My favorite part of Facebook ads is scaling, because now you can take your winning product and blow it up massively. You want to reverse engineer your profit goal for the month when you find a winning product. Find out how much you need to spend per day to hit your profit goal. How much daily revenue and what ROI and ROAS you need to hit. Always reverse engineer from your profit goal.

Below I'll be revealing my most powerful scaling methods. Be warned—these methods may or may not work for you. You must test them all to see what works best. When you do find a method that works for you, you will want to increase your credit card limits, and your Facebook ad spending limit. At peak sales, you'll be spending thousands per day on ads because, at this point, the more you spend, the more you'll make. Cash flow is critical with scaling.

The last problem you will want to have is that you couldn't scale up because your credit card got maxed. Although this sounds like a great problem to have, when you get to that point, you'll be kicking yourself that you didn't manage your cash flow correctly.

DOUBLE UP METHOD

Let's begin with the Double Up Method. What you want to do is double the budget every three days. That's very moderate scaling for this method. If you want to be more aggressive you can double the budget once per day, in the morning. You could literally go from a $20 to $40 to $80 to $160 budget in a matter of days on an ad set. Make sure you never increase the budget after twelve noon. Increasing budget in the morning is a best practice and will yield the best results.

MIRROR IMAGE METHOD

Next, let's cover the Mirror Image Method. With this one, you duplicate your best ad sets daily with different budgets. You can dupe a winning ad set 3–10 times daily, at a maximum. You can test lower budgets like $20, $40, and $60. Also, test higher budgets like $80, $250, or $500. Make sure your audiences are large for this method—over 5 million. That way you won't be competing against yourself, but you'll have max penetration into your target audiences.

REV UP METHOD

The next method is called the Rev Up Method. This is very aggressive scaling. It's kind of like day trading, so use it with caution. You've been warned.

It works a lot better in Q4 for the gift-buying season, so be very careful with this one. So what you do is double up the budget at nine a.m., twelve p.m., and five p.m. Literally, double the budget three times per day. If it's working well, and you're getting high ROAS like 3x or 4x, you can keep doubling it, to a maximum of three times per day. You should also bring the budgets back down the next morning, just to be safe. Be very careful with this method, and only use it in Q4. It's very aggressive, and you can spend a lot of money very quickly.

BREAKOUT METHOD

Next up is the Breakout Method. This one is powerful. You look at the breakdown in Ads Manager to see what type of placements and devices are performing the best, giving you the highest ROAS. Break those segments out into their own ad sets. An example of this would be Phase 1, duping out to mobile Facebook News Feed only. Then you could also try Instagram by itself in another ad set. In Phase 2, you can try desktop News Feed, right hand side only. Then in Phase 3, you break out specific devices like iOS versus Android.

INTL EXPANDER METHOD

The last one is the INTL Expander Method. You start with the US, then you duplicate all your best ad sets over to other countries. Try Canada, Australia, New Zealand, the UK, and Ireland first. Then test Germany, Mexico, Spain, France, Sweden, Switzerland, Denmark, and Norway. These are proven and profitable countries to scale out with your winning product.

ACTION PROMPTS

1. Find your Facebook pixel in Ads Manager and place it in your CommerceHQ admin settings.

2. Launch at least five ad sets per product at $10 budgets. Run for two days to get data. It takes 20–30 products tested on average to find one gold or silver winner.

3. Once you find a winning product, it's time to scale up. Start

by launching 10–20 ad sets per day and split test larger budgets by duplicating your best ad sets.

4. Build up data in your custom audiences so you can create lookalike audiences. LLAs are the most profitable type of ad set, and will make it so much easier for you to scale campaigns.

THE OUTSOURCING OF TASKS

THE MANAGEMENT
OF FULFILMENT

I n this phase, we'll go over fulfilment and customer service and why you'll want to outsource them as soon as possible. These are the two biggest 'time sucks' in an Ecommerce business model. Fulfilment and customer service include repetitive tasks that you can easily train a virtual assistant to do for you. This frees up your time to do more important things like finding winning products and scaling ads.

Let's start with the management of fulfilment. This is part of your business' backend. This is just as important as the front end, but often gets overlooked, because it's boring. When you start scaling your ads and the sales start rolling in, you will need to stop jumping up and down and realize that those profits aren't yours until you fulfil your orders.

Here are the fulfilment rules for your business.

FULFILMENT TIMELINE

All orders from a particular day must be processed on the following day. Do not wait even a few days to process orders, because that can cause a massive backlog, especially if you're shipping products from

China to the US. It's going to be a two-week average shipping time, so you don't want to waste any time or your customers will not be happy. Make sure you're getting tracking numbers back from vendors quickly. If it's taking them five days or longer, you should find a new vendor that ships out faster. If an order is damaged or lost in transit, the vendor should cover this and ship out a replacement immediately.

VENDORS

You need to make sure the vendor who is fulfilling the product is on top of it. Get them on Skype or WeChat for daily communication. Make sure they are well stocked and ready for a big increase in volume. Every couple of months you should be negotiating with your vendors to get pricing down. You can also improve product and shipping package quality to impress your customers so they come back for more.

CSV FILES

You can also set up custom CSV files with CommerceHQ. You would simply export all the orders from the previous day and email over the CSV file to your vendor so they can fulfill. Then in two to three days, they're going to send back to you the tracking numbers for those orders.

SHIPSTATION

Shipstation allows you to buy and print shipping labels. This is perfect for faster shipping times, because you can take all orders from yesterday and package them together into one shipment from China to the US in two to three days. Once they hit the docks in LA, each order parcel will already have their shipping labels attached and be sent off to your customers with USPS. Meaning you can greatly increase shipping times from two weeks down to one week or less. You will get fewer refunds and chargebacks by shipping within a week. And you will get more repeat buyers because of the good experience they had with your store.

TRACKING NUMBERS

It's best practice to send tracking numbers to customers on a request basis only. If they get their tracking before there is any update or change in the shipping history, they will email complaints. Give them their tracking number once their shipment has movement and is en route.

THE CUSTOMER EXPERIENCE

The second most time-consuming task is customer service. The customer experience involves several points of contact. There's email, phone, and Facebook fan page comments. Most stores tend to ignore their customer feedback and experience, because confused or angry customers are a hassle. But Facebook collects user feedback and can rank your store higher or lower, depending on how you're handling your customers. A happy customer might become a repeat buyer, which is how you can get the most out of your store at scale.

EMAIL

Let's talk about emails, and how important they are for your business. Most customers will get in contact with your company through email. Thankfully, there aren't many variations in the questions they will ask, but you should still outsource customer support right after you find a winning product and begin to scale.

Most emails you get sound like this:

- Where is my order?
- What is my tracking number?

- My order is damaged, and I want a refund.
- I have a question about the product.

Because most customers ask the same or similar questions, you can help speed up replies by creating scripted responses for every type of question or issue. Then, when you are ready to hire help, you can give a list of frequently asked questions to your customer service reps.

When you scale up, customer service tickets will increase very suddenly and they can easily pile up. If left unanswered, your customers will escalate by asking for refunds and calling their banks to chargeback. Make sure you have a team ready before you scale to handle the influx of customer service tickets.

It's imperative that you respond to all customer service tickets or requests within 24 hours. Do not make your customers wait, because then they will likely just ask for a refund, and you don't need those headaches in your business. Always make sure your customers are happy, because if they have a good experience with your store, they will come back and buy again.

You can also offer discounts and replacements. But I recommend that before you ever consider doing a refund, offer 20% or 30% off their next order instead. Or you could send out a replacement product. Refunding is the last thing you want to do, the worst-case scenario. Try to be diplomatic and win back the customer's business. If possible, only refund the shipping portion of their order if they're complaining a lot about shipping times.

Also, it's important to have a very low charge-back rate with Stripe or any merchant processor, including PayPal. You must have a charge-back rate below 1%. If not, you risk potentially getting shut down, so you'll be unable to make sales and collect revenue.

PHONE

A phone number makes your store look more legitimate, but you don't want to pay for a phone salesperson, especially when you're just starting out. The best compromise is setting up voicemail. You can get a 1-800 number from Grasshopper.com so people can leave voicemails with their name and email. Have your staff reply to the customer by email. Email is easier to deal with, especially if a customer is very angry.

FAN PAGE MANAGEMENT

For fan page management, it's critical you handle comments on all your ad posts the right way. You never want to delete comments from ad posts, because that can hurt your engagement score. But you can hide them if they are negative and hurt your brand.

What I recommend is replying to negative comments professionally. See if you can truly help them change their mind about your business. Think about it—if someone walked into your brick-and-mortar store, you wouldn't kick them out just because they said something negative about it. You would talk to them and ask what the issues were to find a solution. You want to do the same with your ad posts. You want to post some blog links or content links on your fan pages two to three times per week minimum. That's going to help lower your ad costs by about 10%.

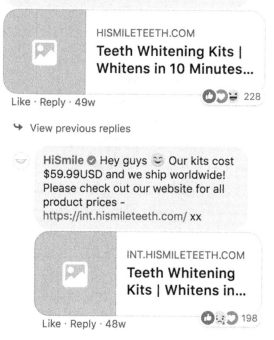

THE FREEDOM IN THE FORMULA

So now we've finished learning how to set up your business. But, this takes up time. Your time. And, as the business grows, you will find yourself running out of hours.

There are two big problems with running your business alone. Number one, you will find it very difficult to scale up. There are only twenty-four hours in a day. And you can only humanly work for eight to twelve of them. You cannot run an entire company by yourself. And if you're ambitious and want a seven-figure company, then you definitely need to buy help. Number two, where's the freedom? You haven't gotten into this industry just to create another 9 to 5 job for yourself. So hiring staff is going to be twofold. Step one: for scaling purposes. Step two: to free up your time.

Now this is not a sexy topic like products, or ads, or scaling. Building a team, managing staff, and setting up systems are not flashy at all. It's not a lot of fun setting up, but once your systems and team are in place, your life will be so much easier.

I will cover who to hire, how to hire them, and when to build your team. This will let you step back as the business owner and focus on working on growing your business instead of doing the day-to-day grind. You'd be surprised how many business owners are in the way of their own company's growth and their own personal freedom. Here are the outsource goals you will need to take your business to the next level.

OUTSOURCE GOAL #1: DON'T GET BURNED OUT

People who try to run their business all by themselves get burned out fast—especially if you are transitioning to entrepreneurship and you still have a full-time job. You might have kids, so there isn't enough time in the day to handle all the tasks alone. You can't find products, launch ads, handle customer service, and do fulfillment once you start scaling. It's not humanly possible. You will need help and to be willing to hand over the keys to your business because, if you are burned out, you are going to make poor decisions. Your goal is to outsource to the point where you can focus on the big picture.

Most storeowners are overworked, under-systemized, and burned out. They try to do everything themselves and can't relinquish control of operations. This can honestly cost you your health, and kill your productivity. Don't be one of those people. You need let go and give control to others so you can focus on growth. Business is a marathon, not a sprint.

OUTSOURCE GOAL #2: LET GO

Please don't be scared of hiring people. It's the only way you're going to grow to the seven-figure level. This is a big thing that people struggle with. You need to have a team mindset because, with more people, you can reach your goals so much faster. Outsourcing is all about buying help--building a team and outsourcing all the work, so that you're not stuck behind a computer screen for eight to twelve hours a day.

You don't even need a big team to get started with scaling your business. You can get massive value from even just one extra person working an eight-hour day. It's very inexpensive. We're talking $2–$3 per hour for most VAs. With just one virtual assistant, you could run a six-figure revenue store very easily. With two to four VAs, you could run a seven-figure store. And if you wanted mid-seven figures, you would need five to seven people on your team. You don't need a team of 20, 30, or 40 people. Bigger teams like that can be incredibly inefficient.

During the busy times, you may have over one hundred customer service tickets or emails to respond to per day. The last thing you want to be doing is customer service; it's a massive time suck and a very negative experience. You started this business to create the lifestyle of your dreams, not to work as a slave on the computer. You have to let go of needing to control everything and know that you can't do it alone.

Think of all the tasks that can be outsourced easily. The key is building an amazing team of talented individuals who can do the repetitive day-to-day responsibilities that allow you to focus on growing your company.

OUTSOURCE GOAL #3: TRUST

New storeowners are sometimes worried about handing over the keys to their business. They have a hard time trusting others to do tasks as well as they can, or are worried they will steal their business. It's nothing to fret about because 99% of VAs or virtual assistants do not have the means necessary to cash flow this type of business. You need high limit credit cards to float and fund ad spend and fulfillment. Plus, if you select the right people from places like the Philippines, you will see just how trustworthy people can be. Without trusting others to help you run the business, you will never be able to scale and grow your business.

OUTSOURCE GOAL #4: HAVE LONG-TERM GOALS

Remember, it can take years, not months, to make millions of dollars in profit. Make sure that you have your sights set properly, and you're not overly ambitious about what you can do in such a short amount of time. You need to have a vision for the long term. You need to know where you want to take your company. How big do you want to grow? How much revenue per year? How many employees? And how quickly do you want to grow at a sustainable level?

Make sure that all your employees are there for a reason, and don't become over bloated. You want to keep company profits high and expenses low.

OUTSOURCE GOAL #5: BUILD AN EMPIRE

Ultimately, you want to build an empire. Most of what you do every day can be taught to someone else. Every time you create a new system for your business, hire it out to someone else, and then create the next system. By stacking systems, you can easily expand your business and create an Ecommerce empire.

For example, if you find a new niche that's selling incredibly well, why not launch another store that's just focused on that niche and list multiple complementary products to your winning product? It's easy to expand with more stores once you have a solid team in place. You can duplicate your success by entering more markets and increasing your reach with new stores.

OUTSOURCE GOAL #6: TAKE TIME OFF

And, finally, take time off whenever you want. You don't have to work every single day. You can work four hours per week if you want to. A project manager can free up a lot of your time to spend with family, travel, or whatever else you prefer doing. There's no need to be at the computer all day long. Don't create another 9 to 5 job for yourself.

THE BUILDING OF A TEAM

There are three options when hiring staff. You could open a local office, you could hire virtual assistants who live in different countries, or you could build an office overseas, where all your virtual assistants work under the same roof.

The US dollar has stronger purchasing power in other countries, such as the Philippines. If we had hired in Canada or America, we would be paying far more per hour for staff. When you're just starting out, it's important for your expenses to be lean. You want most of your investment to be going towards ad spend.

So that's why we built an office in the Philippines for just $5,000. Some Ecommerce businesses have their remote staff working in different countries. But we wanted our staff to work under the same roof. I've heard other businesses struggle with their VAs not communicating with each other or sometimes not getting along. In our office, we have ten people, and it works great as a hybrid method. Our staff can easily switch roles and get information they need straight away, which really helps at scale. You can even hire people from within your employees' families, because they will be local in their hometown. You can hire siblings or significant others and have them work in the same office together.

THE HIRING PROCESS

As soon as you feel yourself getting overwhelmed with work, it's time to hire. You're going to start by going on Upwork.com, the easiest way to get started building your team. The website has tons of trustworthy and experienced people from all around the globe. When reviewing their profiles, focus on work hours, success rate, and reviews. If they look great, send them an instant message through Upwork and then interview them on a Skype call.

The most important thing you are looking for when hiring is attitude. Candidates have got to be super excited about the position, the company, and the industry. In the interview, ask them about their work experience, and get them to tell you about difficult scenarios that happened in the past. This will help you understand how they deal with problems, how they overcome obstacles, and how they find solutions. Also, be sure to ask them about their greatest strengths and weaknesses.

If the interview goes well, you can assign a difficult task for them to complete before fully taking them on. See if they can figure out the task on their own, which will indicate if they are a self-starter. Make sure that you're clear on their schedule, their work hours, and what communication will look like on a daily basis. They need to speak English well. That's key. Luckily, a lot of people in the Philippines are excellent English speakers.

After hiring a new team member, give them thirty days to get up to speed, to become an expert with their daily tasks. It's sink or swim. If they're taking up more of your time than needed, then let them go, because the whole point is to buy help to free up your time. Your employees shouldn't be asking you a ton of questions every single day. They should be able to make decisions on their own to move the ball forward.

FIRST AND SECOND HIRE

Your first hire should handle all the fulfillment and customer service, because that's such a massive time suck for you. Don't spend too much time on that. It's not a good use of your energy. Your first hire is going to wear two hats. Their first task is doing fulfillment, dealing with your vendors, and uploading tracking numbers. Their second task will be answering all your customer service email tickets. Your VA can also come up with 'canned' responses, which you can double check and approve. This will speed up the time needed to reply to tickets.

Your second hire should also focus on fulfillment and customer service. Or you can have one person on fulfillment and another on customer service only. You'll hire this second person after you've scaled up, and the first VA notifies you that they need assistance.

THIRD HIRE

Your third hire should be a social media manager. This person will manage all your fan pages, ad posts, and messages in your inbox (fan pages). This can easily be handled by one person. Their obligations will include hiding negative comments on your ads and answering questions from prospective customers about the product. As your store grows and you add more products, there will be more fan pages and more ad posts to manage.

FOURTH HIRE

The fourth hire should be for ads management. We call this person a media buyer. Their entire job is to launch ads, optimize, and scale. But you will be doing these tasks yourself for the first few months. Once you have a good grasp of Facebook ads, you can train someone to do all the hard work for you on that side of the business.

Hiring a media buyer is very exciting, because launching ads is very time-consuming. What you'll be looking for in a media buyer is someone who has experience with paid traffic. Maybe they've run Google ads before, and maybe even Facebook ads, but they should have a grasp of paid traffic, to some extent. They should be analytical and not emotional at all. They must be numbers-driven and good with math. And they must be willing to take smart, calculated risks. They have to know when to scale up and when to scale down. They must not be scared to spend. They must have a good understanding of targeting, optimization, and scaling. Don't hire a media buyer until you fully understand Facebook ads.

FIFTH HIRE

Your fifth hire should be a project manager. This person will manage your entire business for you, dealing with your employees, and finding new products to launch. It's important to have a consistent pipeline of new products that you are testing. You should have at least one winning product that you're scaling per month. The project manager will help you with that.

Your PM takes charge of your entire team. The team members will report to your PM, and your PM will report to you. They should have direct visibility into your business on a daily basis. What are the leaks in your business you could be improving for better results? A project manager will get a salary plus commissions or bonus pay each quarter. They must be able to hit sales targets each month. Your PM should have excellent people skills and easily build relationships with others. You want to have someone who's personable and who can work well with your team.

Your PM will take the time to build trust and rapport with your team. People always come first because if people aren't happy in your team, there can be performance issues. Your PM will be able to leverage relationships with your team to solve problems that you may not even be aware of. They are on the front lines and must be able to pivot fast when things don't go as planned. If you're trying to scale a product, and after a week or two it's not working, the PM can say, "Hey, you know what? This isn't working. We have to test more products and find a new winner that's actually scalable." Your PM should be able to make those decisions and suggestions on the fly.

They must be comfortable with things changing very quickly or moving in different directions. Their job is to test, fail, then correct to succeed. And that takes time. You need someone with a lot of patience who respects your team's time and feelings, never losing their cool. They must always be professional and should have at least two to five years of work experience. A PM's job is to take ideas from you, flesh out the plan, and assign the tasks to your team.

If you say, "Hey, I want to find a new winning product. Here are some that I found—go test all these products, get the ads launched, and let me know how it goes," their job is to go and assign all those tasks out to the team. They must be persistent about tasks and milestones that make up the plan or goal. The PM needs to request things from multiple people multiple times to accomplish a goal. Your PM is your brand ambassador. They build rapport with the team and outside vendors. They should be able to make small talk and ask how their weekend was, what's going on in their lives, whether they're happy, and whether there are any issues that need to be fixed. Your PM should be asking the team weekly whether there are any roadblocks or any issues that can be adjusted internally to speed up results. And they should always look to optimize business processes. Your PM should question all systems and processes continually and determine how you can do things better and faster by managing from the middle.

Your PM may need to jump in and help team members with certain tasks. They must have the ability to wear multiple hats just like an entrepreneur. They must be self-sustainable and figure things out on their own.

All these people will help you manage, optimize, and scale your business. You want to start new hires with simple, small tasks to build up their confidence and give them easy wins. Do not micro-manage. Let them create systems on their own based on your instructions. Let them try to make your systems better, or come up with their own methods in terms of documentation, tracking, and spreadsheets. You want to trust them in their decision-making process. They're professionals. They have a lot of experience. You must be able to relinquish control so they can help you grow.

THE TOOLS TO KEEP YOUR TEAM ORGANIZED

There are several ways to stay organized with your business and your team. Don't be that entrepreneur who wakes up late, scrambles to put out fires, and is all over the map when it comes to daily tasks. You want to be able to set targets and goals, communicating with your team on a daily basis. This will keep everyone on track and sailing in the same direction.

OFFICE SPACE

You may not want to invest in an office space when you first start out. But once your business is up and running, you should ask for photographs of your team's working conditions. You'd be surprised how many VAs work on lawn chairs or in stuffy rooms with poor internet speed, like this picture:

After you start profiting, you'll want to give your team access to a comfortable workplace. Our office in the Philippines was built on stilts, because the area is prone to flooding. Wherever your staff lives, keep up-to-date with their weather forecasts, as power outages can affect their ability to work. We bought new computers, office desks, and chairs, and pay for high speed internet service. This helps them get their tasks done faster, which is really important when you're trying to scale up your business. You don't want your staff waiting around for pages to load, especially when you're paying by the hour.

Team-building trips are great for morale. These things help immensely, because we're all human, and we're running a human-to-human company. We also buy them snacks, and even do 'pizza Fridays.' We celebrate birthdays with bonuses, and when we do well at the end of a quarter, we give them commissions. Take care of your team, make sure they're happy, and they will perform incredibly well for you. After all, these guys are helping you achieve your dream lifestyle.

VIDEO TRAINING

In terms of training your team, give them step-by-step demo videos for each task. Once you are ready to outsource a particular task, simply record a video showing them exactly what to do and send it off to them. You should be able to perform the task first with success on your own before outsourcing it, especially with Facebook ads.

You can record your desktop using software like ScreenFlow and then upload the video training to YouTube.

COMMUNICATION

Regarding communication, we've found the best app to use is Slack. com. This is by far the most powerful tool, and it is much more organized than Skype. You can create different channels for each part of your business, such as products, ads, fulfillment, and customer support. Invite the team into each individual channel where it makes sense. What's great about Slack is that all the files and links will be easily searchable.

FLASH REPORTS

You want each team member to report daily to your PM or to you. You can use something called a flash report, which is just a simple summary of what they accomplish daily. It will show you what each team member did for the day, and ensure the ship is pointing in the right direction. Make sure to hold bi-weekly meetings, at a minimum.

VIDEO CALLS

Video calls are best, so that you know they're there and that they're paying attention. Everyone must attend the calls, and everyone gets a chance to speak for a few minutes each. The calls should be very high level, and thirty minutes in length, max. You want to discuss what they've done the past week, what they're doing now, and what the plan is for the following week. Skype or Google hangouts work great for this.

HUBSTAFF

What about tracking their work hours? You don't want to use Upwork to track your team's hours, because they charge a 10%

fee. Instead, use Hubstaff.com for tracking, then pay your team via PayPal weekly. This will save you some money, which helps the bottom line. Hubstaff is great because it automatically takes screen shots every few minutes, and even shows you what websites they've visited. You can set weekly limits as well. (Make sure you turn off idle time, because you don't want to be paying them for long breaks, or when they watch movies or TV.) Hubstaff gives you real-time monitoring and visibility into what your team is doing daily, which is great, because you aren't physically in the office with them.

Source: hubstaff.com

TRELLO

In terms of task organization, I find that the simplest app to use is Trello. It uses cards and boards, which you can move around for the different stages of your campaigns. It's super easy to manage things visually, to see where each campaign is at a glance. Tasks like finding products, listing them on your store, and launching video ads to find a winner can all be tracked in Trello. It also helps with ongoing daily checklists, so team members know what they should be doing daily, weekly, or monthly. Each virtual assistant should have their own board with task cards. It's a very efficient way to manage your business and staff.

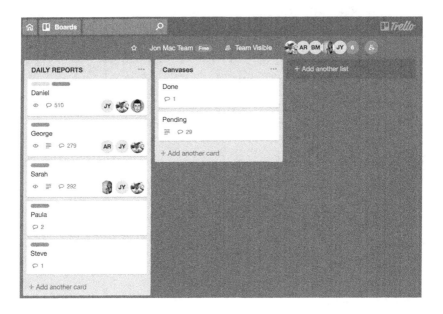

Source: trello.com

SOPS

Let's talk about SOPs, or standard operating procedures. You want to create SOPs for every part of your business. Define the goal for the task, note who will be doing it, and list the apps or resources needed for completion. List the exact steps, and optimize your procedures over time, so that they're faster, easier, and more efficient. Be sure to train everyone on every single SOP as well. You never know when someone will get sick or go on vacation. Everyone should know how to do everything in the business, just in case.

If anyone on your team is away for any reason, you can easily swap roles with someone else to make sure there are no gaps or leaks in the workflow. SOPs should include the title, name, date, description, and the steps, in either image or video format.

Best practice is to record your screen with video while performing the task. Then give the video to your team and have them create the SOP documentation. That's the best way for them to learn the task as well. They are not only watching it but also writing it out. "I do it, we do it, then they do it". As Benjamin Franklin once said, "Tell me and I forget. Teach me and I may remember. Involve me and I learn."

MEETINGS

Try to have at least one company retreat per year, where you meet everyone face-to-face. This will build truly meaningful relationships with your team and have more impact on your business. Don't work while on the retreat. Instead, brainstorm cool new ideas for your business and enjoy each other's company. The best way to create company culture is to build relationships with each other that last a lifetime. Try doing fun activities and tours at exotic places to boost team morale.

THE PROMOTION PLANNER

t's time to plan out your year. A lot of people don't do this, but it's critical that you and your team know what you want to accomplish in the next twelve months. You need to know what's going to bring growth and consistency to your business. Write down your top three goals for the next twelve months to get crystal clear on what you want to happen. Do you want to make a million dollars in revenue this year? How many winning products will you need to find? How much will you have to spend on ads? Reverse engineer your goals. Mapping out campaigns and offers for holidays will help you get ahead of the curve. There are so many opportunities for campaigns, like Valentine's Day, Mother's Day, Independence Day, summer sales, and Halloween, with the biggest being Black Friday, Cyber Monday, and Christmas.

GOOGLE CALENDAR

Set up a simple Google calendar to map out the year. Plug in everything from promotions, offers, and campaigns, to team retreats, and holidays. Don't overcomplicate it. At first, just do a brain dump, get it written down. Just get it written down. Design the lifestyle of your dreams by being super organized and having goals set up over the next twelve months. Be as specific as possible when planning, and organize everything by day, week, month, and quarterly goals. Yes, some things don't always go to plan, but having an idea of where you are going will put you in a proactive state rather than a reactive one. It also helps your team understand the company goals when you have something to refer back to.

EMAIL MARKETING CAMPAIGNS

You can run weekly content or email marketing campaigns to your buyers' list and start offering them promotions for all the special days mentioned. Focus on one winning product per quarter, or stack two or three products at the same time for massive results. Send out weekly email promotions to your list based on the different events that are happening during the year.

JANUARY

National Blood Donors Month
1 New Year's Day
6 Epiphany
15 Martin Luther King Jr. Day

FEBRUARY

Black History Month
American Heart Month
1 National Freedom Day
2 Groundhog Day
4 Super Bowl
12 Daylight Savings Time Begins
13 Mardi Gras
14 Ash Wednesday
14 Valentine's Day
16 Lunar New Year
19 President's Day

MARCH

Women's History Month
National Nutrition Month
1 Holi
17 St. Patrick's Day
20 National Ad Day
29 National Mom-and-Pop Business
    Owners Day
30 Passover Begins

APRIL

Sexual Assault Awareness Month
Autism Awareness Month
National Volunteer Month
1 Easter
7 Passover Ends
17 Tax Day
19 Get To Know Your Customer Day
22 Earth Day
25 Administrative Professionals Day
26 Take Your Children to Work Day
27 Arbor Day

MAY

Asian American Heritage Month
Jewish American Heritage Month
Mental Health Awareness
National Bike Month
5 Cinco de Mayo
7-11 Teacher Appreciation Week
8 Teacher Appreciation Day
13 Mothers Day
15 Ramadan Begins
28 Memorial Day

JUNE

LGBT Pride Month
Men's Health Month
Brain Awareness Month
5 World Environment Day
14 Ramadan Ends
17 Father's Day
19 Juneteenth

JULY

National Cell Phone Month
4 Independence Day
19 Get To Know Your Customer Day
22 Parents Day
30 International Day of Friendship

AUGUST

Back to School Events
National Family Fun Month
Children's Eye Health Safety Month
National Immunization Month
7 National Night Out™
12 International Youth Day
19 World Humanatarian Day
22 Eid
26 Women's Equality Day

SEPTEMBER

Hispanic Heritage Month
National Food Safety Month
3 Labor Day
9 National Grandparents Day
9 Rosh Hashanah Begins
11 Rosh Hashanah Ends
18 Yom Kippur Begins
19 Yom Kippur Ends
28 Native American Day
29 National Coffee Day

OCTOBER

Arts & Humanities Month
AIDS Awareness Month
LGBT History Month
Dental Hygenie Month
Breast Cancer Awareness Month
1 Child Health Day
8 Indigenous People / Columbus Day
14 National Dessert Day
18 Get To Know Your Customer Day
27 National Diversity Day
31 Halloween

NOVEMBER

Indian American Heritage Month
Movember
Adoption Awareness Month
4 Daylight Savings Time Ends
6 Election Day
11 Veterans Day
15 America Recycles Day
22 Thanksgiving Day
23 Black Friday
24 Small Business Saturday
26 Cyber Monday

DECEMBER

World Aids Month
Universal Human Rights Month
12 Chanukah Begins
24 Christmas Eve
25 Christmas Day
26 Kwanzaa
31 New Year's Eve

Source: oaaa.org

AD CREATIVE CAMPAIGNS

Black Friday and Cyber Monday are the biggest sales weeks of the year. Here are some great examples of ad creative. You want to offer deep discounts like 75% off.

HOLIDAYS CREATIVE

Christmas sales are the next biggest promotion of the year, after Black Friday and Cyber Monday. Here's a great example ad that capitalizes on the holidays. This is when the big guns come out. You'll have more competition, but way more sales, revenue, and profit. Fight for sales by stacking power offers like 'buy 3 get 1 free,' '75% OFF,' and 'free shipping.' Hammer offers until they can't say no, or else you will lose out to other advertisers who are going after the same traffic.

Kitchen Tools
October 11 at 5:57 PM · 🌐

🍪 Want to make lovely cookies for Christmas? 🍪
🎇 FREE Shipping!!
🔥 ONLY TODAY 50% OFF 🔥

GET YOURS NOW!! 😍 😍
http://bit.ly/2EcS9wo
http://bit.ly/2EcS9wo

👍❤️ 29   5 Shares 1.1K Views

THE BOSS YOU
ALWAYS WANTED

When you become your own boss, it's easy to forget what it was like to have one! You get so busy with the 'day to day,' that you might end up being the very thing you used to hate. Being a boss is being a leader. A role model. Someone who brings out the best in their team and isn't afraid of getting into the trenches. Don't rule by fear, but by example.

As you train your team, analyze what they excel in and prepare to make each team member an expert in their field. This empowers them to be proud of their position within the company. Give your team a goal to be top of class.

EDUCATE

Invest in their education, their experience, and their success, so that they can grow their skills. For example, our current PM started as our t-shirt designer. He actually wasn't the best designer, but his attitude was so positive. He had an aptitude for learning, and a drive to be successful. I knew he was special. When given the chance, he proved far better at launching ads and training others. Which is why, at only twenty-one, he became our project manager and runs the entire team. Give your team extra training where possible, so that they can grow by thinking outside the box. You never know what secret strengths they have that can be applied to other parts of the business.

COMMUNICATE

Set communication as a routine business ethic. Daily, you will ask for the store ROI report. Weekly, you will ask for the products to be tested for next week, and if there were any bottlenecks in the business. Monthly, you'll explain the store expectations and goals, so that everyone's on the same page. Quarterly, review their systems and processes to maintain efficiency. Get on a Skype call with them and analyze how they're spending their day, and see exactly what they're doing. Look at what their systems and processes look like currently and how you can improve them.

CHALLENGE

You should be setting milestones for each employee: daily, weekly, monthly, quarterly, and yearly. Once hired, move them up to positions of more authority and responsibility. Always try to promote from within. It's much easier to train up an existing employee to a new role rather than searching for someone brand new who doesn't know your business.

DO NOT INTIMIDATE

Mistakes in your business will happen. Fulfilment may fall behind. Margins might be calculated wrong. Money will be lost. And your instinct will be to find the culprit whose fault it is. You might want to dock their pay, or scold them publicly. But guess whose fault it actually is? It's yours.

You're the captain of the ship now. You are the leader. If a staff member isn't pulling their weight, you have to decide whether this is a teaching moment or a firing moment. And most of the time, people can be taught, if they have the right leadership. Do not run your company by intimidating your staff or treating them poorly. Remember what it was like to have a boss and look to your superiors for guidance. If they make mistakes, talk to them privately and figure out how to resolve it together. Teams don't work best when they are nervous about taking a wrong step. It's stifling for creativity, and nobody wants to communicate to a boss they're afraid of.

Keep an open door policy, and if mistakes are made, show by example how to fix them. Concentrate on moving forward, and be the boss you always wanted!

ACTION PROMPTS

1. Hire your first VA using Upwork.com. Their main role will be to handle fulfillment and customer service for you so you can focus on launching ads.

2. Once you start to scale up your business, you will need more help. Hire a second and third VA, and give them one role each so they can master their tasks.

3. After you hire three or more VAs, consider bringing on a project manager to direct and communicate with your staff daily.

4. Last, hire a media buyer to launch ads for you, optimize, and even scale. When you get to this point, your time working in the business will be a lot less, so you can focus on business growth, month after month.

PHASE TEN

THE FUTURE
OF ECOMMERCE

THE NEED FOR A
DIFFERENT PLATFORM

Let me tell you about my Ecommerce platform, CommerceHQ. I'd like to explain why I felt it was necessary to bring another Ecommerce platform to the industry.

CommerceHQ was born out of frustration with the available Ecommerce platforms out there.

THE SHIPPING PROBLEM

Shipping products from China to the US, on average, takes about two weeks with ePacket but, with Amazon Prime, people can get their orders in two days or less. So customers now expect faster shipping times for the products they order online.

CommerceHQ has solved this problem with a built-in seven-day shipping app. It allows you to buy and print shipping labels for all your customers' orders so you can ship them in two days via air. Then once the parcels reach the US, they all have their own shipping labels and are sent out for delivery and arrive at your customers' doorsteps within two to five business days. This whole process takes less than seven days and solves the slow shipping problem from China, without you having to open a warehouse, hire local staff, or buy inventory. Faster shipping will increase your conversion rates, average order value and get you more repeat buyers.

THE COMPETITION PROBLEM

Branding is critical in order to stand out amongst the competition. To maximize this opportunity and make it easier for you, we developed a revolutionary Visual Builder app right inside CommerceHQ. It allows you to drag-and-drop elements to design and create a store that is uniquely yours. You can even modify our best themes to your heart's content. Imagine being able to create single-product, long-form sales letters with images, videos, reviews, and more. The possibilities are endless with our Visual Builder app. You can also create full funnels with ease, allowing you to double or even triple your average order value by upselling similar products to customers before and after they check out. This one app changes everything and will evolve the Ecommerce industry like no other.

THE THIRD-PARTY APP PROBLEM

Other Ecommerce platforms charge you an arm and a leg for third-party apps that can slow down or even break your store. Every second more that it takes to load your website can reduce your conversion rate by 10%. I don't think it's fair for these massive corporations to be nickel-and-diming you for every little app and feature you need to succeed with your store. For this reason, we build the most commonly used apps right into CommerceHQ so that everything is seamless, neat, and easy to operate. Conversions rates can double when you use CommerceHQ because our system is so optimized and fast loading. You will save thousands per year by not having to pay for expensive third-party apps.

THE FEES PROBLEM

Other Ecommerce platforms charge you a percentage of your

revenue—anywhere from 2% to 4%, which I think is highway robbery. CommerceHQ will never charge you transaction fees. Keep your profits to yourself and reinvest them in your business. It's amazing how greedy some of these other platforms can be. We only succeed when you do and want to give you the maximum bang for your buck. With CommerceHQ, you'll get 10x the value of any other platform on the market for a much lower operating cost.

THE CONVERSION RATE PROBLEM

CommerceHQ was built from the ground up to convert higher than any other platform in the world. We know what sells and what works online. We understand buyer psychology and know what it takes to make a sale. With a combined 25+ years in sales and marketing, my business partner, Vlad, and I have put all our experience into the platform. This is why you see people's conversion rates literally double overnight simply by switching to CommerceHQ. Our apps and themes are all designed to get you more revenue and profit for your store.

THE TIME-TO-SET-UP PROBLEM

You can have your store up and running the same day you create your account with CommerceHQ. Everything comes out of the box ready to go. No need for developers or coding. With just a few clicks of the mouse, you can be set up to start making sales and taking payments with your online store. The process is a breeze, and we have the best customer support in the industry. We will not sleep until you are satisfied with the software and are happy with your new store. Remember, the record speed for a store setup is five minutes and nine seconds.

If you are ready to launch your store, or move over to the highest converting platform in the world, sign up now for your free fourteen-day trial: https://CommerceHQ.com, and I'll see you on the other side!

THE ECOMMERCE TRAJECTORY

Ecommerce has only just begun. In terms of all retail sales, Ecommerce is currently pegged at just 12% market share, and has increased by 3.5% in the past decade. Brick-and-mortar stores are still the dominant player in a big way, but that means there is a ton of room to grow for Ecommerce. There are massive opportunities for new online stores to compete against traditional brick-and-mortar stores.

You don't have to worry about market saturation or competition; there is more than enough to go around. We are still 38% away from reaching 50% retail market penetration. Ecommerce millionaires are being minted year after year, as technology makes it easier to build, launch, and scale your online store.

Why do people shop online to begin with? Because of the convenience, selection, and speed of shopping. As every year passes, people want access to special products faster and faster. They don't want to drive down to the local mall, try to find parking, and wait in lines to get what they want. Ecommerce alleviates all these issues and makes for a wonderful buying experience, all done from the comfort of your own home.

What does the future hold for Ecommerce? Automation. You

will start to see more and more automation with the software and tools you use to sell products online. Wizards that guide you through the setup process of listing products and launching ads will become commonplace. Optimization of your store will also be automated in terms of design, product placement, and website structure. With a push of a button, you will be able to fine tune your Ecommerce business. Automation software will suggest what to do next, so you are never stuck at a revenue ceiling.

Personalization of the online shopping experience will be a driver of Ecommerce growth in the future. More than ever, people want offers crafted and targeted just for them. They want personalized suggestions for other products that they might like or be interested in. Machine learning, a form of automation, will allow this to become a reality. As algorithms progress, data becomes more powerful to mine, optimize, and action.

In the future, branding and single-product page stores will be the norm, and an absolute must have if you want your business to thrive. Every product you promote will be its own brand, with images, videos, logo, testimonials, upsells, and cross-sells built-in. By directing potential customers through a hyper-focused product funnel, you will be able to double or even triple your average order value to maximize profits.

Regarding Facebook ads, costs will rise as more advertisers flood the platform. But Instagram will be the next big traffic and sales opportunity for the future of Ecommerce. And Facebook ads give you direct access to Instagram for ad placement. Instagram stories will be extremely popular, and molding your ad creative to fit this ad unit will be vital to your success.

To alleviate rising, paid traffic costs, content marketing will play a big part in building massive lists for your online stores. Capturing the lead will be the entry point of the funnel for future follow-up and sales closing of the product, through email funnels and sequences. Customers will engage more with content pieces like blog posts, video tutorials, and networking groups to create a community feel around your products. User generated content will play a big part in this strategy.

Digital products will be a perfect companion to physical products with your store. You will be able to upsell your customers into training, coaching, and advice membership portals, related to their niche.

International traffic and sales are still very untapped. McKinsey & Company (an American worldwide consulting firm) reports that 1.4 billion people will join the middle class worldwide in the next two years alone. Asia Pacific will dominate 85% of those 1.4 billion people. You will be surprised how much revenue potential is overseas. And you can reach them with Facebook ads easily.

Ecommerce has been the greatest opportunity in the past decade. It's never been a better time to be alive. Do not take this for granted. Get on the Ecommerce train before it's too late. The pioneers and early bird entrepreneurs will reign supreme by taking advantage of technology, reach, and marketing. Sell or be sold to. There is no other option. Take the bull by the horns and just do it! I can say, without a shadow of a doubt, that Ecommerce is here to stay and has a very bright future ahead.

THE CONCLUSION: YOUR INVITATION

Congrats, you made it! You've learned how to build, launch, and scale your Ecommerce business. Thank you for sticking with me during this journey. I know that was a lot of information to take in, so I suggest you read the book several times and take notes. Feel free to review each chapter as you start your Ecommerce empire, step-by-step.

Now that you've finished reading the book, what will you do with all the knowledge, strategies, and techniques you've learned? What type of store are you going to launch? Which niches and products are you going to run campaigns to?

Are you ready to start (or continue, if you've been working along with each chapter) your journey to financial freedom?

The fact is, you could read this book many times over, but unless you take immediate action, everything you just learned will go to waste. Also, it's important not to get "shiny object syndrome" and move on to the next trend or business opportunity. Focus is paramount, and you need to put in the time to make this business work. Work hard, but work smart. Outsource whenever possible. No problem or barrier is too difficult to overcome.

Simply search Google or YouTube to find answers and advice on nearly any topic.

I'm challenging you right now to get your store up and running within the next thirty days. I know you can do this! Imagine starting to make sales this month! How would that change your life? You will finally be able to quit your job, spend more time with your family, and be your own boss. You will be able to live your dreams right now instead of when you retire at sixty-five or later.

The time is now to make a massive change in your life. But it takes perseverance, focus, and determination to succeed. Never give up! Keep pushing through your obstacles. Celebrate your successes early on to keep yourself motivated.

Use your responses to the action plans at the end of each Phase. Your goals should include tasks such as launching your store, researching products and niches, creating your Facebook ad campaigns, or finding a coach or mentor to help you with your business.

FREEDOM FORMULA BUSINESS PLAN

Write down ten business goals you will achieve within the next thirty days. Allow this book to be your cheat sheet to help you through every step of your Ecommerce journey and earn your freedom.

Now that you have a plan in place for your business, consider how to pass on this knowledge to your friends and family, or perhaps find a partner to help you launch. You now have the exact blueprint we use in our business to earn seven figures every single year. It's a strategy guide to help you earn revenue and profit quickly. But you need to believe in yourself and have a vision for your business. Always know where you want to go, and chart a course to your goals. If you need direct help, I can offer you a complimentary thirty-minute strategy call to help you get on track and make sure you're building out your new business properly from day one. Apply here for a call with me: http://jonmac.co/apply. Include your name and time zone so we can coordinate your strategy call via Skype.

I hope you learned a great deal and are motivated to take action to achieve your ultimate life goals, dreams, and aspirations!

I hope this is just the beginning of our journey together, and that I can personally help you in the future with training, coaching, and live events. I enjoy teaching, and I love changing people's lives. Maybe you will be next!

Finally, I hope you found what you were looking for in this book. I wish you all the luck, success, love, happiness, and prosperity that life has to offer.

Now get out there and sell something!

SUCCESS STORIES

From Stalled At $380k To $8,600,000

- Jonas Hedegaard

- Business was stalled at $380k/year

- Now Doing $716,000/month

- Having to cut back on advertising because the business is getting a bit too big and they have to make some key new hires before ramping back up

- $700k months are now predictable & expected

From stay-at-home mom to millionaire

- Isabel Pizarro

- 1-woman entrepreneur making $1,300,000/year while raising children

- Now makes $300,000/month with less work and more predictability

- Within one year grew her business into the millions

From zero to $820,000 in 90 days

- Jack Scanlan

- Rolled out this system and made $820,000 in the first 90 days

- Had to STOP ad spend because there was too much volume for his team to handle

- Is putting together a system and team to handle the volume and will be at 8-Figures this year

From chaos to focused and $250,000/month

- Juan Florez

- Business was stalled at $15,000/month

- Now doing $250,000/month and growing

- Has mastered Facebook Ads with our proven system

From struggling to $500,000

- Chris Santos

- Business was struggling, over spending on ads

- Online store was not optimized for conversion

- Within 3 months grew to $500,000 and scaling

Tyler S. Miller is 😄 feeling thankful.
November 30 at 11:03am

In May 2017, I purchased Store Formula and CommerceHQ. Since then, my store has done over $1M in sales! This has been so life changing for me and my family. 🔥

I am very pleased that I made the smart decision to go with CommerceHQ for my e-commerce platform of choice. Here's a few reasons why:

☀ This one deserves to be at the top: SUPPORT! CHQ support is amazing. Some of the fastest response times I've ever seen. ... See More

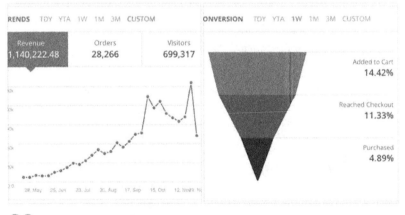

😊👍 You, Isabel Pizarro, Alan Young and 56 others   15 Comments 1 Share

Tetiana Kolienko
January 24

Hi everybody! Last months were absolutely amazing. Since August to this day we made with ONE product, ONE CommerceHQ store almost $1.1 million in sales! 😊

We would like to share our story. Beginning was super hard! We first started completely blind without any training or anything and we were just losing money everyday.. 😕

So couple months ago we decided to fly to USA and attend Jon Mac's Millionaire Challenge. I need to say it completely opened my eyes and changed my understanding of how to sell, pick products and run this business. 😲 What we learned from Jon Mac and other people was absolutely awesome. Couple weeks after that we created our first store, we dumped our old store (that never worked anyway) and just moved completely to CommerceHQ.

Basically we picked niche, first products, created store with very simple design to not paralyze people when they are scrolling through store (we basically used default CommerceHQ theme). Then we begin filling store with products and launched couple campaigns. First 10 products were absolute fail 😕, we were barely break even. However we didn't quit and pushed more hard and product no. 12 was absolute winner. 💪😎 Since that day we were able to scale it to $20,000 in sales per day. 😱 Usually we were running around 2 ROAS. Actually scaling and optimization were easy, we used all optimization rules Jon recommended in his event (I think they are in CommerceHQ video bootcamp from last week as well).

I already know 2018 will be best year of our life! 😊

👍 Like   💬 Comment

 Steven Snider, Isabel Pizarro and 89 others

Grant Alexander
June 6 at 1:04am

Well it's been quite the journey since August 2017 for me. All I had was $1000 bucks and never give up attitude. I've faced all the pit falls of this business, but always knew that if I stuck at it i'd eventually save enough money to get my 1 on 1 time with Jon Mac. That day finally came and I extend my deepest gratitude for everything he has taught me. This is now a new beginning for my business and it's in these times I am so very thankful I stuck at it. Big Thanks to Jon Mac and his team for everything you do 🙏

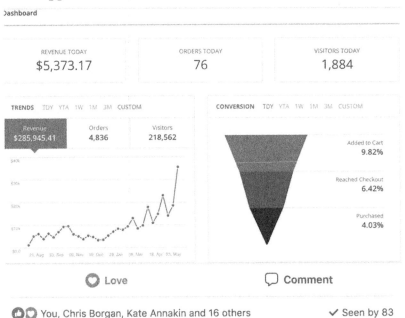

⭕ Love   💬 Comment

You, Chris Borgan, Kate Annakin and 16 others   ✓ Seen by 83

Chris Santos
January 5 at 3:58pm

2017 Results - (6 Months) 884K in Revenue. This was a lot of work and I am very excited to share this with everyone. I will be working extra hard in 2018 to reach my first 7 figures and scaling from there!

Setting larger goals than you think you can do is essential. Testing fast and scaling fast is too 🙂 I had to leverage every ounce of credit 💳 I had and when the money 💵 came back in, it was reinvested and the ad spend went back up 📈!

There are so many nuggets that can be sh... See More

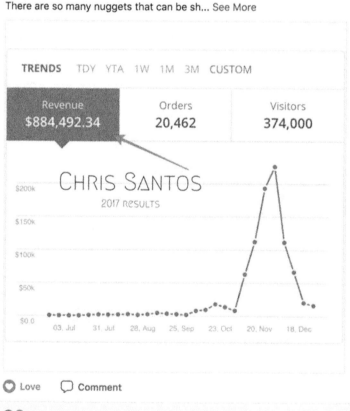

💙 Love   💬 Comment

👍❤️ You, Robert Cole, Kate Annakin and 66 others

Jack Scanlan is with Jon Mac.
16 hrs

Store Formula was what really helped me put the pieces together with my ecommerce business. I had a store that was making money before, but once I implemented what I learned in Store Formula, the system really started to explode.

The main things that I was missing were the systems and automations to get my business moving along smoothly. The most important system, was the ad automation section. Once I put my ads in a system, my roi went way up! And the next most important system was my team. Once I learned how to delegate and automate my business, I was able to spend less time on tasks, and more time planning. This allowed me to scale faster, grow bigger, and really build a brand.

Jon has a special way of taking you by the hand and showing you exactly how to follow a proven system. His training is clear, and concise, and most importantly, actionable. And if you follow along, you will make money!

I have had my best quarter ever this first quarter of 2018. And I am well on my way to $5million in revenue this year! Thank you Jon!

👍 Like   💬 Comment

😊😍 Isabel Pizarro, Amish Shah and 24 others

BLUE LABEL CONSULTING

Feeling overwhelmed by all the information in this book? Gain clarity and begin your journey with Jon personally in his new program, Blue Label Consulting.

Jon has taken several people from zero to seven figures within months, and you could be his next success story! Get unlimited access to Jon via email on a monthly basis and watch your business grow to seven figures and beyond. Jon will simplify the process for you, help you optimize your business, and guide you to choose winning, profitable products right from day one. This will potentially save you tens of thousands of dollars wasted on testing. Let Jon show you the way and give you all his best strategies that are proven to work in the current marketplace!

If you want personalized, one-on-one help and coaching from Jon Mac, contact him directly at jonmac.co/apply. However, Jon's time is extremely limited, so he can only take on a certain number of students each year. So if you want to skyrocket your success by running your own Ecommerce store and have Jon support you the entire way, book a call with him now!

For more information, visit http://jonmac.co/apply

Aymeric Monello is 😋 feeling thankful with Ray Donnelly.
November 14 at 1:38 PM

Exactly 2 years ago, I discovered Jon and the Store Formula.
Unfortunately, I didn't put enough effort in because I had another
business that was taking all my attention and the venture died.
Fast forward two years and my team and I are very excited to see a
tremendous growth following our calls with Jon within the Blue Label
consulting in as little as two weeks! You'll find below a couple of
screenshots to illustrate what I'm talking about.
Thank you Jon for showing us the way and for giving us this opportunity.

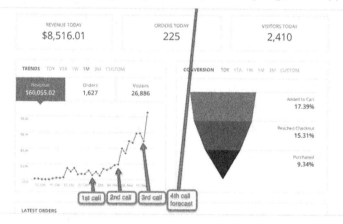

Travis Ashley
October 22 at 1:24 PM

I'd like to share my progress so far in Q4, working one-on-one with Jon and his Blue Label Coaching Program. Hopefully it serves as good Monday Motivation 💪😎 for anyone questioning their abilities. Here's to continued growth and learning! 📖😄

Blue Label Coaching - 2 Week Progression

1. Struggling to test and find winners
2. Blue Label Sign-Up
3. Found 2 Potential Winners
4. First Coaching Call With Jon
5. Up..Up..and Away!!

👍❤️😮 Minh Van Le, Jonas Hedegaard and 33 others   11 Comments

Lynn Fetch
September 21

STOP WASTING YOUR TIME!

I took a leap of faith and finally invested in myself as I'm smart enough to know when I need help but stubborn enough to be trouble:)

I joined Blue Label w/Jon one month ago and it was the BEST decision I've made since starting my biz. I had hit a wall with my store and was having trouble scaling and staying consistently profitable.

Jon was Awesome! He understood my goals and where I wanted to go and was so patient with me and all my questions.. For me, people need to stop wasting all their time with other 'gurus' and just focus and stick with Jon. He literally took one glance at my ads manager and knew exactly what to do and how to fix, plus gave me actionable tasks to do that immediately returned results Day 1.

Since my coaching with Jon my store revenues and ROI have both increased 3X in just 30 days!!! It's so exciting to see this growth and turn a corner. I now have systems in place that I can continue to build on and power me through Q4.

Thanks Jon and Team- looking forward to what the future brings:)

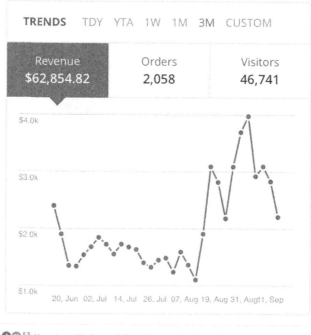

You, Jonas Hedegaard, Eyad Ghazzawi and 32 others   3 Comments